Words Their Way™

Word Sorts for Syllables and Affixes Spellers

Third Edition

Francine Johnston
**University of North Carolina, Greensboro,
Associate Professor Emerita**

Marcia Invernizzi
University of Virginia, Professor

Donald R. Bear
Iowa State University, Professor Emeritus

Shane Templeton
University of Nevada, Reno, Professor Emeritus

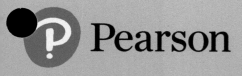 **Pearson**

330 Hudson Street, NY, NY 10013

Editorial Director: Kevin Davis
Portfolio Manager: Drew Bennett
Content Producer: Yagnesh Jani
Portfolio Management Assistant: Maria Feliberty
Development Editor: Carolyn Schweitzer
Executive Product Marketing Manager: Christopher Barry
Executive Field Marketing Manager: Krista Clark
Procurement Specialist: Deidra Smith
Cover Design: Taylor Reed, Cenveo
Cover Art: Pearson Education
Editorial Production and Composition Services: iEnergizer Aptara®, Ltd.
Full-Service Project Manager: Victoria White/Rakhshinda Chishty
Printer/Binder: LSC Communications
Cover Printer: LSC Communications
Text Font: Palatino LT Pro

For related titles and support materials, visit our online catalog at www.pearsonhighered.com

Library of Congress Cataloging-in-Publication Data

Names: Johnston, Francine R., author. | Invernizzi, Marcia, author. | Bear,
  Donald R, author. | Templeton, Shane, author.
Title: Words their way : word sorts for syllables and affixes spellers /
  Francine Johnston, Marcia Invernizzi, Donald R. Bear, Shane Templeton.
Description: Third edition. | Boston : Pearson, [2018] | Includes
  bibliographical references.
Identifiers: LCCN 2017018247 | ISBN 9780134530710 | ISBN 0134530713
Subjects: LCSH: English language—Orthography and spelling—Problems,
  exercises, etc. | English language—Suffixes and prefixes—Problems,
  exercises, etc. | English language—Syllabication—Problems, exercises,
  etc.
Classification: LCC PE1145.2 .W67 2018 | DDC 428.1/3—dc23 LC record available at
https://lccn.loc.gov/2017018247

11 2021

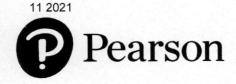

ISBN 10:   0-13-453071-3
ISBN 13: 978-0-13-453071-0

Contents

OVERVIEW

Word Sorts for Syllables and Affixes Spellers is a companion volume to the core text *Words Their Way: Word Study for Phonics, Vocabulary, and Spelling Instruction*. The core text supplies the theory and research that underlie the curriculum laid out in these companions, and it is important that teachers have this text available for reference. This book provides prepared reproducible sorts and step-by-step directions for guiding students through sorting lessons. There are organization tips as well as follow-up activities to extend the lesson through weekly routines.

The collection of sorts in this book is designed for students in the syllables and affixes stage of development—students who are usually in the upper elementary grades and middle school (grades 3 through 8). Students who spell most one-syllable words correctly have the foundational knowledge needed to spell the base words to which affixes (both suffixes and prefixes) will be added. They will also be ready to look for familiar vowel patterns in two- and three-syllable words. It is important that students not begin the sorts in this collection until they have a firm foundation in vowel patterns within one-syllable words. To figure out exactly where individual students should start, you need to administer one of the spelling inventories described in Chapter 2 of *Words Their Way*.

Word study as we describe it is analytic. Students examine words they already know how to read, and sometimes even spell, as a way to develop generalizations about how the spelling system works. This in turn enables them to decode and analyze unfamiliar words they encounter in reading and to master the spelling of similar words. For this reason, we do not recommend that you give a pretest and then eliminate all the correctly spelled words from the weekly routines and the final assessment. Known words provide important reference points for the student who is using but confusing the spelling feature of interest. In this way, we help students work from the known to the unknown through the scaffolding process to arrive at conclusions that will help them as readers and spellers. However, you may want to use pretests at times to determine if students are appropriately placed in the word study sequence. Students are expected to spell between 50% and 75% of the words correctly on the pretest if the words and features are at their instructional level.

SCOPE AND SEQUENCE OF THIS BOOK

The third edition of *Word Sorts for Syllables and Affixes Spellers* includes 58 sorts and is divided into nine units with 1,300 words. First, students will learn how to add inflected endings (*-ed, -ing, -s*) to words using the "double, drop, or nothing" rule. Two-syllable words will be introduced through compound words, and then students will study the pattern of vowels and consonants at the place where syllables meet. We call these *syllable juncture patterns*. Next, the long-vowel patterns that students studied in the within word pattern stage will be reviewed in the stressed or accented syllable of two-syllable words. In a similar fashion, *r*-influenced and ambiguous vowels (e.g., *oy, ou, au,* and *aw*) will also be reexamined in two-syllable words. After studying stressed syllables, students will look at the unstressed syllables that occur most commonly at the end of two-syllable words (e.g., *-el* or *-le*).

You may be familiar with and prefer the term *syllable types*, which is another way of describing how individual syllables are spelled. There are six syllable types: (1) closed—the syllable is "closed" with a consonant, usually though not always indicating a short-vowel sound as in *pan or panic*; (2) open—the syllable is "open" because it ends with a long-vowel sound as in *me* or *o-pen*; (3) vowel-consonant-*e* as in *make* or *bite*; (4) vowel team as in *team* or *cloud*; (5) *r*-controlled as in *mark* or *north*; (6) final stable syllable—this includes

1

the frequent "consonant-*le*" pattern (*table, cycle, buckle*) as well as other common, final, unaccented syllables (*nation, creature, label*). All but the final syllable type are already familiar to students who have completed the sorts in the within word pattern stage. Talking about syllable types may be more helpful in Unit V than trying to apply knowledge of syllable juncture patterns.

Later sorts cover some of the unusual consonant sounds and spellings, such as hard and soft *g* and *c*, *k*, *qu*, and silent consonants. The final sorts introduce words with common prefixes (*re-, un-, dis-, pre-*, etc.) and suffixes (*-y, -ly, -ness, -ful*, etc.) that affect the meaning and usage of words in straightforward ways. The study of syllables and affixes anticipates the more complex Greek and Latin roots and affixes that are explored extensively in the derivational relations stage. This collection of sorts ends with a look at homophones and homographs. (**Note:** As part of your vocabulary instruction, you may wish to address some of the roots in the earlier sorts in the Derivational Relations supplement. Students should not be expected, however, to spell correctly all of the words used to illustrate these roots.)

The sorts in this collection present about 24 words each week, a larger number than many spelling programs, but they are grouped by spelling features that make them memorable. The words have been selected according to their frequency of occurrence in reading materials for the elementary grades as well as their potential for developing generalizations about the spelling system. Students are expected to spell the 24 words in the sort and understand the spelling principles that the sorts reveal. Plenty of words are needed to discover generalizations and to compare patterns and features. If you feel that 24 words are too many, however, you can, in most cases, reduce the number by simply cutting off the last row of words. However, we believe that if students are appropriately placed, work with the words throughout the week, and use the routines we recommend, 24 words are not too many, especially when they are grouped by spelling features. As mentioned above, if students are properly placed in the word study curriculum, they should already be able to spell many of the words, so they will not be learning 24 completely new words in each lesson.

RESOURCES AND ORGANIZATION TIPS

Each unit begins with a section called Notes for the Teacher, which provides placement guidelines and background information about the features of study.

The section describes extension activities, and it includes a unit spell check that can be used as pre- or posttest. Each lesson offers suggestions to guide the lesson with questions that engage students in critical thinking and reflection. Sorts can be introduced in a number of ways, and the way you choose depends on your own teaching style as well as the experience of your students. Many of the sorts in this book are set up as teacher-directed sorts with the categories already established with headers and key words. These sorts work well when you are introducing a new unit or if you feel that your students need more explicit modeling and explanation. However, if you wish to make word sorting into more of a constructive process in which students discover the categories, you can cut off the headers before distributing the word sheets and use student-centered sorts to engage students in more active thinking.

Sorting is an essential instructional routine even for students in the upper grades who still enjoy the opportunity to manipulate words as they look for patterns and relationships among them. Word sorts are presented here as blackline masters that can be reproduced for every student to cut apart and use for sorting. Enlarge these about 10% before making multiple copies to reduce cutting and waste. Prepare your own set of words for modeling on a tabletop, pocket chart, or projector, enlarging them as needed. Some teachers create sorts to be used on interactive whiteboards, tablets, and other digital equipment. Teachers often share these resources, but be aware of copyright laws that prohibit making sorts available electronically to unauthorized users. Any teacher using these sorts should own a copy of this book.

It is important that students sort their own words several times throughout the week or during the lesson time frame. We recommend that the cutting of the sort for the week occur during noninstructional time, such as during the daily arrival routines of hanging up jackets and attendance. Some teachers hand out individual sorts after the introductory lesson to be cut apart back at student desks. Students should be directed to personalize their word cards before cutting. They might write their initials on the back of each word, but the quickest way to personalize the sort is to draw three colored lines down the back of the handout. Each student should be assigned a different color of crayon to draw a line through the middle of each column. If you need more colors, simply combine two (such as blue and orange). Thus, when words end up on the floor (and they certainly will), they can be identified and returned to the owner.

Words can be stored each week in plastic bags or envelopes for repeated sorting and can be taken home for additional practice.

Digital Resources

A number of digital resources can be found at the PDToolkit for *Words Their Way*. You can use the Custom Sorts Tool to create a digital version of the sort that is timed and gives corrective feedback. Just enter the headers and words from the blackline master sorts contained in this book. The sorts can be saved and used at any time by students to practice on a computer. Students enjoy timing themselves, and you can set an accuracy level and speed that you want them to achieve in their sorting. The games and sorts on the PDToolkit designed for this stage can be downloaded and printed to use. Also available are assessment tools and videos of teachers working with students in small groups and sharing their experiences with word sorting and organization.

PLACEMENT

Word Sorts for Syllables and Affixes Spellers, Third Edition, contains nine units of study that are grouped by early, middle, and late designations in the table of contents. Following are general guidelines for placing students using the inventory results.

Early syllables and affixes spellers know how to spell both long vowels and other vowels in single-syllable words on the Elementary Spelling Inventory (ESI) or the Upper Level Spelling Inventory (USI) but will make two or more errors when spelling inflected endings. They are ready to explore in depth the generalizations that govern when to drop a final *e* or double the final consonant before -*ed* and -*ing*. If students are still missing two or more features under vowels or complex consonants, they will benefit from the sorts for late within word spellers offered in *Word Sorts for Within Word Pattern Spellers*.

Middle syllables and affixes spellers spell inflected endings correctly on either the ESI or the USI, but they make mistakes under syllable juncture and unaccented final syllables. They are ready to examine vowel patterns in two-syllable words, issues of syllable juncture, and accented and unaccented syllables.

Late syllables and affixes spellers spell most words correctly under syllable juncture and unaccented final syllables (missing no more than two) and are transitioning into the derivational relations stage,

spelling many affixes (prefixes and suffixes) correctly. They will benefit from the study of the most common prefixes and suffixes in words that are easier in terms of spelling and meaning than the prefix sorts in the next supplement, *Word Sorts for Derivational Relations Spellers*.

ONGOING ASSESSMENT

Pre- and Posttesting with Unit Spell Checks

Most units in this book contain spell checks that can be used as pretests to gather more in-depth information about features and to place students more accurately. For example, you might give the spell check in Unit I to students who are in the early syllables and affixes stage to determine if they can spell words with inflected endings. If students spell 90% on a spell check correctly, then you can safely move on to the next feature. If students spell between 50% and 75% of the words correctly on the pretest, then the words and features are at their instructional level and they will benefit from completing all the sorts in the unit. This leaves a gray area between 75% and 90% that requires teacher judgment. Consider factors such as your own observations, the nature of the sorts, and grouping dynamics. It is not always possible to place students exactly where they need to be and still have a manageable number of groups. (We recommend three or four groups at most.) If students score less than 50%, earlier features generally should be studied first.

Ideally students will score at least 90% when the unit spell check is given as a posttest. If they do not, consider the errors students make. Some reteaching might be needed, or you might let students advance to the next unit while observing to see how well they perform. Sometimes the next unit will provide review, in which case moving students on, even with scores less than 90%, is advised so that they do not "stagnate" on certain features. It is especially important to set a steady pace with students who are struggling and below grade level in order to let them catch up and supply them with the skills they need to succeed.

Goal-Setting Record Forms

We have provided a form on the next page (see Figure 1) that teachers and students can use to monitor progress. There is a place for pretest and

FIGURE 1 Syllables and Affixes Speller Goals

		Student	Teacher		Date		
	Unit Spell Checks	Sorts and Features	Weekly Tests	Sorts and Features	Weekly Tests	Sorts and Features	Weekly Tests
UNIT I Inflected Endings	Pretest date	2. adding -ing: double		3. adding -ing: double and e-drop		4. review	
	Posttest date	5. adding -ed		6. unusual past tense		7. adding -es	
		8. unusual plurals		9. y + inflected endings			
UNIT III Syllable Juncture	Pretest date	13. VCV and VCCV		14. VCV and VCCV		15. VCV and VVCV	
	Posttest date	16. VCCCV and VV		17. open and closed syllables + endings			
UNIT IV Long-Vowel Patterns in Accented Syllables	Pretest date	18. long a patterns		19. long i patterns		20. long o patterns	
	Posttest date	21. long u patterns		22. long e patterns		23. review	
UNIT V Other Vowel Patterns in Accented Syllables	Pretest date	24. oy/oi and ou/ow		25. au, aw, and al		26. r-influenced a	
	Posttest date	27. r-influenced o		28. w or /w/ before vowel		29. er, ir, ur	
		30. ure, ear, and eer					
UNIT VI Unaccented Syllables	Pretest date	31. le		32. le, el, il, al		33. er, ar, or	
		34. agents and comparatives		35. (/chur/ and /zhur/)		36. en, on, ain, in, an	
	Posttest date	37. et, it, ate		38. final -y, -ey, and -ie		39. y + inflected endings	
		40. a-, de-, be-					
UNIT VII Exploring Consonants	Pretest date	41. initial g and c		42. final c and g		43. more words with g	
	Posttest date	44. /k/ spelled ck, ic, and x		45. gu		46. silent consonants	
		47. gh and ph					
Unit VIII Affixes	Pretest date	48. re- and un-		49. dis-, mis-, and pre-		50. non-, in-, and fore-	
	Posttest date	51. number prefixes		52. -y and -ly		53. -er and -est	
		54. -ness, -full, and -less					

posttest scores from the unit spell checks, places to record weekly assessment scores, and a list of sorts and features that can be checked off.

Students can chart their own progress on weekly assessments and spell checks. This can be very motivating and encourages students to be responsible for their own learning. Students who are struggling in spelling may feel overwhelmed with all they need to learn, but defining a set of limited goals can be helpful. We recommend that you meet with these students individually and share the results of the unit spell check given as a pretest. Then identify the goals for the unit stated in the first column, or more specific goals such as completing just one or two sorts if you are setting a faster pace. Each week, students can record their weekly test scores. You may need to do this together for a few weeks until students are familiar with the form. At the end of a unit, they can take the unit spell check as a posttest to see the progress they have made. The form can be stapled or pasted into students' word study notebooks.

Teachers may keep their own copy of a form for each student and use it in a similar fashion.

We recommend that you check off the features mastered on the pretest using one color of pen or pencil as a way to identify the features that need to be studied. The posttest results can be checked off in another color. This will make it easier to analyze the pretest results if you are trying to determine whether or not students need to complete the entire unit or skip some sorts for a faster pace.

PACING

The series of lessons in this book are designed for an introductory pace. With 58 lessons, these sorts will take about two school years to complete, typically beginning in third grade and extending into fourth and even fifth grade. We supply a pacing guide in Figure 2 to help you make decisions based on assessments and knowledge about your students. We do offer one caveat: When students are far behind their peers (perhaps scoring in the early syllable and affixes stage in fifth or sixth grade), it is important to use a moderate or even advanced pace to move them along as quickly as possible.

FIGURE 2   Pacing Guide for the Syllables and Affixes Stage

	Introductory Pace	Moderate Pace	Advanced Pace*
UNIT I Inflected Endings	Sort 1 is optional. Complete Sorts 2–9.	Skip Sorts 1–3 and 7.	Complete Sorts 4, 5, and 9.
UNIT II Compound Words	Complete Sorts 10–13.	Do one or two sorts.	Unit II is optional.
UNIT III Syllable Juncture	Complete Sorts 13–17.	Skip Sort 13.	Use Sort 17 to review open and closed syllables.
UNIT IV Long-Vowel Patterns in Accented Syllables	Complete Sorts 18–23.	Assess to determine what lessons are needed. Review with Sort 23.	Review with Sort 23.
UNIT V Other Vowel Patterns in Accented Syllables	Complete Sorts 24–30.	Complete all the sorts.	Assess to determine what lessons are needed.
UNIT VI Unaccented Syllables	Complete Sorts 31–40.	Complete all the sorts.	Assess to determine what lessons are needed.
UNIT VII Exploring Consonants	Complete all the sorts.	Complete all the sorts.	Complete all the sorts.
UNIT VIII Affixes	Complete all the sorts.	Optional sorts: Use to introduce affixes with easier vocabulary.	Skip these sorts and go on to the derivational relations sorts.
UNIT IX Miscellaneous Sorts	Sort 55 is optional. Complete Sorts 56–58.	Sort 55 is optional. Complete Sorts 56–58.	Optional, but Sort 58 is recommended.

*Use unit spell checks to determine what sorts students need.

After introducing a sort, you should spend about a week using routines that encourage students to practice for mastery. If your students seem to be catching on quickly, you can increase the pace by spending fewer days on a sort or you may skip some sorts altogether. On the other hand, you may need to slow down and perhaps even create additional sorts for some students using the blank template in the appendix to this book. Additional words are included for most sorts to provide more practice or to challenge students with a more developed reading vocabulary. Although these sorts are arranged in a sequence that builds on earlier understandings, there may be a few cases in which you decide to use the sorts out of order. Some of the prefix sorts, for example, can be used earlier than what we present here. Additional sorts and words may be found in the appendix to *Words Their Way* as well as online at the *WTW PDToolkit*.

WORD STUDY ROUTINES FOR SYLLABLES AND AFFIXES SPELLERS

In most classrooms, students work with their words over the course of a week to ensure that they have the practice necessary to learn generalizations and secure words in memory. Standard routines usually begin with the introduction to the sort on Monday, resorting and follow-up activities scheduled throughout the week, and an assessment on Friday. In addition, there are other activities that we describe as "optional." These optional activities vary depending on teacher preference, time available, and the nature of the sort itself. Throughout this book, you will find suggestions for specific extensions depending on the sort. Word study notebooks are a convenient way to organize student work. Schedules, routines, and activities are described in detail in Chapter 3 of *Words Their Way*.

Standard Lesson Routines

Generalizations are stated for each sort as a guide for teachers. Do *not* begin a lesson by stating the generalization for the students! Instead use the sort and suggested discussion questions to help students tell you generalizations in their own words. Word study is about guiding students to make discoveries about words that they can then generalize to other words. Telling students what they need to know robs them of the opportunity to discover it on their own.

Exploring Meaning: For many lessons, we have listed words whose meaning should be discussed either before sorting or after sorting (if students begin by sorting independently). Some of these may be unfamiliar to students (e.g., *perplex*) or may have multiple meanings (e.g., *quiver*). Invite student input and be ready to supply student-friendly definitions, illustrations, or sentences to support understanding. Small drawings and short definitions could be added to the word cards by the students themselves to help establish meaning.

Dictionary practice is important, and word study lessons offer many chances to extend students' dictionary skills during the syllables and affixes stage. Dictionaries should be grade appropriate. One we recommend is the *American Heritage Children's Dictionary* with students in grades 3 to 6. Despite the ease of using digital dictionaries, begin with paper dictionaries, which are often colorful and appealing. Start by modeling how to look up and interpret dictionary entries for a few words as part of the introductory lesson. Then begin to ask for volunteers to look up just one word in a dictionary in advance of the lesson to later report to the group. Keep these discussions of word meanings brief, but revisit word meanings on other days and assign tasks like using words in sentences or illustrating them as word study notebook activities: *Write a sentence about something that has recently perplexed you. Draw a picture of the quiver you'd carry and one that shows something that would make you quiver.*

Reading Through the Words: Students cannot successfully sort words they cannot read, so review the words quickly before sorting in the group. If there are one or two words that prove difficult to read, set them aside during the initial sort. Bring them back after students have reached some conclusions and use them to apply the generalization in figuring out the new word. For example, students might stumble on reading the unfamiliar word *tranquil*, but after examining how *qu* works in the familiar words *request*, *equal*, and *frequent*, they will then be able to decode it.

Sorting: Students will benefit from small-group lessons during which they have a chance to sort the words and talk about what they can learn from the sort. When you are introducing students to sorting, or when you are introducing a new feature or a challenging sort, we recommend a **teacher-directed sort** that begins with modeling and collaborative sorting. However, once students are familiar with sorting and with categories, we recommend an

open sort that students do independently. In an open sort cut the headers off the handouts (but keep them to use later) to get the most thinking from your students. They will enjoy the challenge of figuring out the categories for themselves. Just be sure to schedule time later to talk about word meanings, review the headers, and reflect on the sort. Suggestions for introducing specific sorts will be offered in the units that follow. Read about different levels of support in Chapter 3 of *Words Their Way*.

Checking: After sorting, check the sort by reading words aloud in each category, using eyes and ears to be sure that the words are placed correctly. Students should then be asked to analyze the words in each category and identify common features. They should identify the oddballs and explain why they do not fit into the established categories.

Reflections and Developing a Generalization: Word study offers a chance to engage students in active thinking. Simply sorting words correctly is not the goal. Sorts are designed to reveal generalizations about how words work, and the reflection part of the lesson should involve students in sharing observations and reaching conclusions through open-ended questions. As noted earlier, do not start a lesson by stating the generalization; instead ask *What do you notice about these words*? Conclude with, *What did we learn from this sort to help us as readers and spellers*? and encourage lots of ideas by probing with *Tell us more*, or *What else did you notice*? Help students shape their ideas into a generalization. At first you should model this and record it for them, but gradually turn over more responsibility to students. Writing their own generalization or reflection can be part of the writing sort described below.

Recommended Follow-up Routines to Extend the Sort

Repeated Work with the Sort: Make a copy of the sort for students to cut apart so they can work individually with the featured words multiple times after the sort has been discussed in the group. Extra sorting and other activities can also be done for homework. A special homework form is supplied in the appendix to this book.

Recording Sorts and Reflection in Word Study Notebooks: Students record their word sorts by writing them into columns under the headers or key words established in the group sort. The multisensory and kinesthetic aspects of writing help secure the spelling of words in memory at the same time students must make decisions about the correct categories. The written record provides a "home base" for the other weekly routines and homework assignments. At the bottom of the writing sort, have your students reflect on what they learned by stating a generalization in their own words. At first you need to model this as part of the word study lesson, but gradually make students responsible for writing their own and add it to the checklist of expectations for the word study notebook.

Blind Sorts and Blind Writing Sorts: A blind sort should be done only after students have had a chance to practice a word sort several times. Model these sorts first as a group activity, and then assign students to work with a partner. Begin by laying down headers or key words. Students work with a partner who calls out a word without showing it. The student points to where the word should go, and the partner lays down the word card to check its spelling against the key word. In a blind writing sort, headers are written at the top of a sheet of paper. The student then writes the words in the correct column as they are called aloud. After the word has been written, the partner calling the words immediately shows the word card to check for correctness. When there are homophones in a sort, the student calling the words must provide a definition. Blind sorts require students to think about words by sound, pattern, and sometimes meaning, and to use the key words as models for analogy. They are a great way to practice for spelling tests and can be done as a group activity or assigned for homework. Blind sorts are not appropriate for some features (such as prefixes) where the category is obvious just from the sound of the word.

Word Hunts: Students should look for words in their reading materials that mirror the featured sound or pattern. These words should then be added to the proper column in their word study notebook. Take time to talk with students about the words they found. Did certain patterns turn up more than others? Could any oddballs be sorted into their own category? You may want to create posters or displays of the words students discover for each category and ask students to reflect on the results. Students can continue to add to these posters over time to continually be thinking about the features.

Assessment: To assess students' mastery, ask them to spell the words using a traditional end-of-the-week spelling test format. You need to call out only 10 to 12 of the words instead of the whole list to save time if you have multiple groups. To check for application of generalizations, you can sometimes call out several words students have not studied (see the list of additional words provided for each sort). Occasionally you may wish to alternate the traditional format with a "sorting" format in which students write the called-out word under the appropriate key or header word. Chapter 3 of *Words Their Way* has forms you can adapt to assess the activities that students complete during the week as well as how they apply their new learning when they write. Also consider assessing students' ability to state generalizations.

When students are placed appropriately in the word study sequence and have adequate time to work with the words during the week, you should see scores of 90% or better on a weekly assessment. If this is not the case, you should first consider whether students are doing something productive with their words every day in school and perhaps at home to master the words and one or more generalizations. You might also reexamine the students' inventory results to determine if they have been placed properly. Some students may need to work on easier features first.

Optional Extensions

Speed Sorts: Repeated and/or timed speed sorts help students internalize spelling patterns and become automatic in recognizing them. After setting up headers, students are timed as they sort their words into categories. After obtaining a baseline speed one day, students repeat the sort several times and try to beat their own time on another day. Many teachers find they can do a speed sort as a quick whole-class activity even though students have different sets of words. Students can also work in pairs using a stopwatch.

Illustrate or Use the Words in Context: Students may be asked to select some words to illustrate or to use some of them (not *all* of them) in sentences to demonstrate the meaning of the words. This is especially valuable for words with multiple meanings and with homophones and homographs. You will need to lay down some expectations regarding the detail in these drawings. Also, you will need to model how to turn simple sentences into more elaborate ones whose context shows the

meanings of the words. For example, show students how they can turn the simple sentence, *I saw a rabbit*, into a more elaborate version, such as *I saw a small brown rabbit hopping through the forest*. Asking questions such as *What kind of rabbit?* or *Where did you see it?* can prompt more elaborate sentences.

Apply Spelling Generalizations: New to this edition are ideas about how to help students apply the generalizations as they develop decoding and spelling strategies. For most sorts, there are additional words that students can be asked to read or spell and then asked to justify their efforts. Spelling strategies that students should develop include:

1. Think of sound and possible spelling patterns. (Two-syllable words have many of the same vowel patterns as one-syllable words.)
2. Try more than one vowel pattern to see which one looks familiar or looks right. (Is it *showted* or *shouted*?)
3. Use analogy or a rhyming word. (If you can spell *yellow*, it can help you spell *fellow*.)
4. Think about the position of the vowel sound. (*Oy* is used at the end of a word or syllable rather than *oi*.)
5. Think of the base word and how it might change before adding suffixes (*skimmed* is *skim + m + ed*).
6. Use a best guess or frequency. (When a short vowel is heard in the first syllable, it is usually followed by two consonants.)

Students (and teachers) may experience some frustration in finding and applying generalizations for some sorts. The answer is not always simple and, to master English, sometimes spellings just have to be memorized. However, thinking about possible patterns for a vowel sound, syllable juncture, frequency, and position will help students narrow the possibilities.

Alternative Sorts: To encourage flexible thinking, ask students occasionally to sort their weekly words in different ways besides the targeted categories. Possibilities include parts of speech, alphabetical order, rhyming words, homophone pairs, and words with silent vowels or silent consonants. Occasionally ask students to think of their own categories.

ENGLISH LEARNERS

Students whose spelling inventory results place them in the syllables and affixes stage of spelling have mastered many of the basic letter–sound correspondences and spelling patterns of English. However, certain features may pose confusion for English learners. For example, double letters, as in *traffic*, are very common in English but not in other languages like Spanish (e.g., *trafico*). Verb forms such as *-ed* and *-ing* as well as plurals and comparatives (*-er* and *-est*) may need to be mastered orally along with the spelling. Compounding words (*lightheaded*, *backward*) and adding affixes to base words (*unhappily*) are common in English but may be rare in some languages. The explicit study of these features and words will be important in helping English learners master English spelling but will also boost both vocabulary and grammar.

Some words in these sorts are likely to be new vocabulary words to English learners, so pay special attention to building knowledge of word meanings and begin the sort with the most familiar words. Because the focus is on the spelling features in most sorts, a full knowledge of all words is not essential, but choose a few words to introduce at any given session and discuss the meaning of additional words each day. There should be many opportunities to use the words in speech and writing.

Students can draw on their other language(s) to learn about the words they do not know. Ask English learners to think of related words, including cognates, in their primary languages. For example, Spanish speakers can see that *adhere* and *adherirse* are cognates. Create a chart of the words that students share, and help students to generate related words and phrases. The websites Onelook and Visuwords may be a helpful source for phrases.

In many cases, pronunciation may be as challenging for English learners as word meanings, so read over words in advance and read the words in columns after sorting. As students work together, English learners hear the pronunciations of their classmates. Reading the words in the lists aloud in small groups also provides reading support. The focus on accent in Units IV, V, and VI will draw attention to a feature that is important for students learning English. In English, most words are accented on the first syllable, while in other languages this is not the case. You can see this in the differences in the accent patterns in the English/Spanish cognates *divide/divider* or *contain/contener*.

General Suggestions for English Learners:

1. Reduce the number of words in a sort by eliminating three to six that are least familiar.
2. Check students' understanding of the meaning of the words and be ready to explain the meaning of three or four words. Use illustrations to support word meanings when possible.
3. Spend extra time using the words in context and discuss their meaning, not only in the introductory lesson but also throughout the week.
4. Pair English learners with English speakers for partner work.
5. Accept variations in pronunciation. (Even native English speakers pronounce vowel sounds in a variety of ways.) Allow students to sort in ways that make sense to them but still reflect sound and pattern correspondences.

Unit I   Inflected Endings
(-*ing*, -*ed*, -*s*, -*es*)

NOTES FOR THE TEACHER
Background and Objectives

Inflected endings are a subcategory of suffixes that indicate tense (*walked, walking, walks*) and number (*cats, foxes*). While we usually talk about generalizations and avoid the term *rules*, we make an exception when it comes to the conventions of adding inflected endings to one-syllable words because they are reliable and straightforward. (See Chapter 7 in *Words Their Way: Word Study for Phonics, Vocabulary, and Spelling Instruction* for a complete listing of rules.) To apply the rules across a variety of words, students will need an understanding of consonant and vowel patterns in the base word. For this reason, the first sort in this unit is a review of vowel patterns that will later determine whether one must drop the final *e* (CVCe as in *hope*), double the final consonant (CVC as in *hop*), or do nothing except add the ending (CVVC as in *rain* or CVCC as in *jump*). Sorts 2, 3, 4, and 5 are designed to help students learn to identify base words and to see how the pattern in the base word must be considered before adding -*ing* and -*ed*. Sort 6 examines irregular verbs (*sleep/slept; keep/kept*). There are many more of these words, and students can be challenged to brainstorm others, find them in word hunts, and create a class list that can be added to over time.

Plurals are introduced in the within word pattern stage but are revisited here in different words. Sort 7 reviews the use of -*es* after certain consonants (*ch, sh, x,* and *s*) and examines how -*es* adds another syllable to a word (*box-es, fenc-es*). Sort 8 examines words that form the plural in unusual ways such as *foot* and *feet* as well as words that end in *f* and change to *v* before adding -*es* (*wife* to *wives*). Sort 9 explores words ending in *y* where sometimes *y* must be changed to *i* before -*s* and -*ed*. After completion of this unit students will:

- Identify base words and the pattern of vowels and consonants in the base word
- Know when to double the final consonant or drop the final *e* before adding -*ed* and -*ing* in both studied words and transfer words
- Know when to add -*s* or -*es* to a base word
- Know how to spell irregular verbs and unusual plurals studied in these sorts
- Know when to change a final *y* to *i* before adding -*ed* and -*es*

Targeted Learners

These sorts are intended for students in the early syllables and affixes stage who can already spell the vowel patterns in the single-syllable base words to which inflected endings are added. Use Unit Spell Check 1A as a pretest to see which of your students are in need of these particular sorts and which features need to be covered.

Teaching Tips

There are several ways that students can be introduced to inflected endings, and other sorts are suggested in *Words Their Way* and at the PDToolkit. Because the inflected ending sorts are designed primarily to teach rules rather than the spelling of particular words, it is important to challenge students to apply the rules to words that are not in the sorts. For this reason, transfer words are suggested for most of the sorts. Word hunts will be especially fruitful when students look for words that end in -*ing* and -*ed* in their reading materials. Words like *king* and *sing* might turn up in a word hunt and will give you the chance to reinforce the idea of base words. However, word hunts for irregular verbs and unusual plurals are not recommended because they are hard to find.

Some understanding of parts of speech—particularly verbs and nouns—will be helpful in talking about some of these sorts. A simple explanation of verbs as words that show action and nouns as people, places, and things may suffice. As we see below, there are also opportunities for mentioning auxiliary, or helping, verbs.

Literature Connection

Explore parts of speech with books such as *Kites Sail High: A Book about Verbs* and *Merry-Go-Round: A Book About Nouns* by Ruth Heller. The books *If You Were a Plural Word* by Trisha S. Shaken and Sara Gray as well as *Fish and Puppies, Thieves and Guppies* by Brian P. Cleary and Brian Gable will go along with Sorts 7 and 8.

UNIT SPELL CHECK 1A PRETEST FOR INFLECTED ENDINGS

Use the unit spell check below as a pretest to identify students who need to study the generalizations covered in this unit. Call the words aloud for students to spell on a sheet of notebook paper. Use the words in sentences if necessary to be sure students hear them correctly.

1. swimming	2. eating	3. fries
4. living	5. fixing	6. stayed
7. dropped	8. foxes	9. helped
10. spelling	11. leaves	12. plays
13. named	14. stirred	15. crying
16. swept	17. wolves	18. watches
19. grabbed	20. humming	

Interpreting Scores on Pretests

Use the goal-setting form on page 4 to analyze and record results. Use the pacing guide on page 5 to plan which sorts to use.

- **90% or better**—Acceptable mastery of inflected ending. Move on to other units. Students will get a review of "double, drop, or nothing" when they do Sort 17.

- **75% to 85%**—A "gray area" where teacher judgment is needed. If you feel that your students only need a review, you can skip the introductory sorts (1 to 3) and focus on the others. Consider the errors students make to determine what is needed. For example, if a student gets all the plurals correct, you can skip Sorts 7 and 8.

- **70% or less**—Students will benefit from doing all the sorts in the unit, although Sort 1 is optional.

UNIT SPELL CHECK 1B POSTTEST FOR INFLECTED ENDINGS

Students should be expected not only to spell words from sorts in this unit but also to apply their understanding of how to add inflected endings to other base words. For a posttest, students are given unstudied base words and asked to add -*s*, -*ed*, and -*ing* using the Unit Spell Check 1B form on the next page. Alert students to the fact that they will need to add two irregular verbs (*said* and *flew*) under "add -*ed*." Model how to use a word in a phrase or sentence to listen for the inflected ending. (Example: *He trips over his own feet. He tripped over the box. He went tripping down the stairs.*)

Students should score 90% or better immediately after the completion of the unit. If students score less than 90% on the posttest, consider the errors students make to determine if reteaching might be needed on the features that students miss.

The final posttest should look like the following:

base word	add -*s* or -*es*	add -*ed*	add -*ing*
1. trip	trips	tripped	tripping
2. chase	chases	chased	chasing
3. need	needs	needed	needing
4. dress	dresses	dressed	dressing
5. dry	dries	dried	drying
6. mix	mixes	mixed	mixing
7. fan	fans	fanned	fanning
8. race	races	raced	racing
9. say	says	said	saying
10. fly	flies	flew	flying

Unit Spell Check 1B   Posttest for Inflected Endings

Name _____

Directions: Add the ending to the base word. Don't forget to look at the pattern and spelling of the base word to determine what changes might be needed.

Base word	Add -*s* or -*es*	Add -*ed*	Add -*ing*
1. trip			
2. chase			
3. need			
4. dress			
5. dry			
6. mix			
7. fan			
8. race			
9. say			
10. fly			

Sort 1 Review of Vowel Patterns in One-Syllable Words

This is an optional sort for students who are not familiar with looking for consonant (C) and vowel (V) patterns. These abbreviations will be important in the discussion and understanding of syllable patterns throughout this book. The category CVCC is introduced here for the first time because it is important to distinguish words that end with two consonants from words that end in one consonant when adding inflected endings.

Generalization: Patterns of consonants and vowels in words can be described as CVVC, CVC, CVCC, and CVCe.

CVVC	CVC	CVCC	CVCe
chief	**wrap**	**smell**	**whine**
fruit	twig	sharp	theme
brief	when	thank	brave
scout	plot	front	scale
groan	clog	climb	phone
stain	quit	trust	quote

Sorting and Discussion:

1. Prepare a set of words to use for teacher-directed modeling. Begin by going over the entire sheet of words to read and discuss the meanings of any unfamiliar words. You can do this by displaying the words on a projector or on a whiteboard, handing out the sheet of words to the students, or going quickly through one word card at a time.
2. Explain, **This is a review of vowel patterns you may have studied earlier.** Introduce the headers CVC, CVCC, CVVC, and CVCe by pointing out that the *V* stands for vowels in the middle of a word and the *C* stands for consonants. Model the sorting of the four boldface key words (*chief, wrap, smell,* and *whine*): **Here is the word *chief*. I see two vowels in the middle and a consonant on each side, so I will put this under CVVC.** Repeat with each key word, pointing out the consonant and vowel patterns

in each word and, if you wish, underline those letters in the key words. Remind students that the single initial C can also stand for two consonants such as the *wr* in *wrap* or the *ch* in *chief*.

3. Say, **Help me sort the rest of these words under the headers.** The words *quit* and *quote* may cause some confusion because the *u* is normally a vowel. In these words, however, *u* represents the /w/ sound acting as a consonant. Contrast *quit* with *bit* or *sit* to help students see that the vowel pattern is CVC and not CVVC because the *u* is part of the *qu* blend.
4. Check and reflect. Encourage reflections by asking, **How are the words in each column alike? What do you notice about the vowel in each column?** Students should note that the words under CVC have short-vowel sounds while the words under CVCC have a mixture of vowels (*sharp, front,* and *climb*). Most, but not all, of the words under CVVC and CVCe have long-vowel sounds (*scout* has a diphthong).
5. After modeling the sort, have students cut apart and shuffle their cards, and then sort using the same headers and key words. After the students sort, have them check their sorts by looking for the pattern in each column. If students do not notice a mistake, guide them to it by saying: **One of these doesn't fit. See if you can find it.** Check to be sure *quit* and *quote* end up in the correct columns.

Extend: Have students store their words in an envelope or plastic bag so that they can reuse them in individual and buddy sorts. Students should repeat the sort several times using the vowel pattern headers, write the sort in their notebooks, and add words from word hunts. See the list of other standard weekly routines for follow-up activities to the basic sorting lesson on pages 6–8 and in Chapter 3 of *Words Their Way*.

An alternative sort would be by long vowels, short vowels, and other vowels. Word hunts will turn up many more words that can be added to these categories. The card game *I'm Out* described in Chapter 6 of *Words Their Way* can be adapted to review vowel patterns. Instead of naming a specific vowel pattern such as *ai*, the leader of a round would name a more general pattern such as CVC.

SORT 1   Review of Vowel Patterns in One-Syllable Words

CVVC	CVC	CVCC	CVCe
chief	**wrap**		**smell**
whine	fruit		twig
sharp	theme		brief
when	thank		brave
scout	plot		front
scale	groan		clog
climb	phone		stain
quit	trust		quote

Sort 2   Adding -*ING* to Words with CVC and CVCC Patterns

Generalization: When a base word ends in a single vowel followed by a single consonant (CVC), double it before adding -*ing*. When a base word ends in two consonants (CVCC), do nothing except add the -*ing*.

CVC	double	CVCC	nothing
get	getting	rest	resting
swim	swimming	yell	yelling
run	running	pick	picking
sit	sitting	stand	standing
shut	shutting	pass	passing
skip	skipping	jump	jumping

Sorting and Discussion:

1. Prepare a set of words for modeling. Set aside the headers for now. Write up or display these two sentences and read them aloud:

   > I don't like **resting** when I can be outside.

   > I am **getting** hungry for lunch.

   Explain, **We are going to learn how to add -*ing* to base words. Look at the word** *resting*. *Rest* (underline) **is the base word. Look at the word** *getting*. **What is the base word? Right,** *get* (underline). **Do you notice anything unusual about the spelling of** *getting*? (An extra *t* has been added before the -*ing*.) **Did this happen to the spelling of** *resting*? No. **Let's sort some words to find out when we double the last letter in the base word and when we do nothing.**

2. Explain, **We are going to begin this sort by pulling out all the base words and sorting them under the key words** *get* **or** *rest*. Select another word such as *yell* and say, **Where will this word go?** (Under *rest*.) **Why?** (It ends in two consonants.) Then say, **Help me sort the other words.** After sorting the base words, ask, **What do you notice about the words in each column?** Talk about the short vowel and the patterns of consonants and vowels. Explain, **Here are headers for CVC and CVCC. Where will they go?** Point out the pattern of consonants and vowels if necessary.

3. **Now let's find out what happens when we add -*ing* to the base word. Here is the word** *rest-ing*. **I will put it beside the base word** *rest*. **Help me match the rest of the words.** Then ask, **What happens to the base word under** *get* **when we add -*ing*?** Explain, **We say that the last consonant** *doubles* **before adding -*ing*.** Put the header *double* above the word *getting*. Then ask, **What happens when we add -*ing* to the base words under** *rest*? Guide them to notice that the -*ing* was just added without any change to the words under CVCC. Add the header *nothing*.

4. Continue the reflection by asking, **What have you learned about adding -*ing* to a base word? When do you double the final consonant? When do you do nothing and just add -*ing*?** If time allows, have students repeat the sort in the group using the headers and key words. Have students check their sort by looking for the pattern in each column. Help them put the generalization or rule into their own words. You may want to write this on chart paper and post it for reference. Leave space for the additional rules and revisions that will develop over the weeks to come.

Extend: Students should repeat this sort several times and work with the words using some of the weekly routines on pages 6–8. For a blind sort, use the headers *double* and *nothing* and sort only the words ending in -*ing*. Tell students to look for more words in a word hunt that have -*ing* added to a base word. Students will find many words that do not fit either of the categories (i.e., *making*, *seeing*). Tell your students to add these words to a third column (oddballs), and challenge them to see if they can discover the rule that governs these other words in anticipation of the sort for next week.

Students can be asked to write contrasting sentences for the base word and its -*ing* form: *I swim on a team. I have been swimming for three years.* Ask students to share sentences using the -*ing* form and ask them if they notice anything (using -*ing* as a verb often requires helping verbs such as *is, am, have been, was,* etc.). For the weekly assessment, call aloud only words with -*ing* added.

Apply: Because this is a rule with wide application, we encourage you to give students new words to apply the generalization. Some suggested transfer words are: *drip, hunt, tug, kick, stir, mop, wink, quit, wish, sob, guess, smell, chop, drag,* and *purr*.

SORT 2   Adding *-ING* to Words with CVC and CVCC Patterns

CVC	CVCC	double	nothing
get	**getting**		**rest**
resting	swim		yell
swimming	skip		run
sit	yelling		skipping
stand	running		pass
sitting	pick		standing
jump	shut		picking
shutting	passing		jumping

Sort 3   Adding -*ING* to Words with CVCe and CVVC Patterns

Generalization: When a base word ends in silent *e*, the *e* is dropped before adding -*ing*. If two vowels in the base word are followed by a single consonant, do nothing except add -*ing*.

CVCe	*e*-drop	CVVC	nothing
write	writing	dream	dreaming
close	closing	moan	moaning
use	using	eat	eating
wave	waving	look	looking
trade	trading	clean	cleaning
skate	skating	mail	mailing

Sorting and Discussion:

1. Prepare a set of words for modeling with the group and set aside the headers. Write up or display the sentences:

    We will be **writing** a report next week.

    Last night I was **dreaming** about the beach.

    Remind students that last week they learned about adding -*ing* to base words with the CVC and CVCC patterns and ask them to recall the rules. Then ask, **What is the base word in** *writing*? **How would you spell** *write*? **What happened to the** *e*? (It was dropped.) Repeat with *dreaming*. **What is the base word in** *dreaming*? **Was there any change to the base word when -*ing* was added?** (No.) **Let's do our sort to find more rules about adding -*ing*.**

2. Students might be asked to sort independently because this sort is similar to Sort 2. For a teacher-directed sort, start with, **We are going to begin this sort by pulling out all the base words and sorting them under either the key words** *write* **or** *dream*. Select another word such as *close* and say, **Where will this word go?** (Under *write*.) **Why?** Then say, **Help me sort the rest of these words.** After sorting the base words ask, **What do you notice about the words in each column?** Talk about the long vowel and the patterns of consonants and vowels. Explain, **Here are headers for CVCe and CVVC. Where will they go?** Point out the pattern of consonants and vowels if necessary.

3. **Now let's find out what happens when we add -*ing* to the base word. Here is the word** *writing*. **I will put it beside the base word** *write*. **Help me match the rest of the words.** Then ask, **What happened to the base word** *write* **when we add -*ing*?** Students should notice that the silent *e* was dropped. Repeat with several more words in the CVCe column. Explain, **We say that the** *e* **is dropped before adding -*ing*.** Put the header *e-drop* above the word *writing*. Then ask, **What happened when we add -*ing* to the base word** *dream*? Guide students to notice that the -*ing* was just added without any change to the words under CVVC. Add the header *nothing*.

4. Continue the reflection by asking, **What have you learned about adding -*ing* to a base word? When do you drop the** *e*? **When do you do nothing and just add -*ing*?** If time allows, have the students repeat the sort in the group using the headers and key words. Have students check their sort by looking for the patterns in each column. Review what students learned in the previous sort and add the new rule to the chart you started last week.

Extend: Students should repeat the sort and do other weekly activities. Go over the words students found in a word hunt last week that did not fit a category and ask students if they can add those to one of the categories from this week. Are there any words that do not go into any of the categories? For the weekly assessment, call only words with -*ing* added.

Apply: Give students additional words and ask them to apply the rule. Some suggested transfer words are: *ride, need, give, bake, peek, smile, vote, bloom, scream, joke,* and *come.*

SORT 3   Adding -*ING* to Words with CVCe and CVVC Patterns

CVCe	CVVC	*e*-drop	nothing
write		**writing**	**dream**
dreaming	close		moan
wave	using		eating
looking	eat		skate
closing	trading		cleaning
clean	use		moaning
trade	skating		waving
look	mail		mailing

Sort 4   Review of Double, *E*-Drop, and Nothing

This review adds another pattern (CV/CVV) as well as some exceptions. If students need only a review of the rules for adding -*ing* and are good at looking for patterns, you might start with this sort.

Generalization: When a base word ends in one vowel and one consonant (CVC), double the consonant before adding -*ing*. If the base words end in a silent *e* (CVCe), drop the *e* before adding -*ing*. Nothing needs to be done to other base words (CVCC, CVVC, or CV). Final *x* never doubles.

double	e-drop	nothing	oddball
setting	**hiking**	**reading**	
cutting	moving	cheering	
stopping	living	spelling	
begging	coming	floating	
grinning	having	growling	
jogging	sharing	talking	
humming		pushing	
		fixing	
		working	
		going	
		snowing	

Sorting and Discussion:

1. Prepare a set of words to use for teacher-directed modeling on a projector, tabletop, or pocket chart. Display all the words and ask, **What do you notice about the words in the sort?** Students should notice that they all end in -*ing*. Point out, if they don't notice that all the words are verbs, that the words name things you can do.

2. Explain, **This sort will review adding -*ing* to base words.** If students have done Sorts 2 and 3, you might let them do this sort independently. Otherwise, for a teacher-directed sort, put up the headers *double*, e-*drop*, and *nothing*. Introduce each key word by asking, **What is the base word in ____? What was done to the base word before the -*ing* was added?** You may want to underline the base word in each key word. Sort one more word under each key word and then sort the rest of the words with student help.

Fixing should be under the header *nothing* for right now.

3. Guide the students to reflect by asking, **How are the words in each column alike?** Talk about the vowels and the pattern of consonants and vowels. Students should notice that the base words under *double* have the CVC pattern and those under e-*drop* have the CVCe pattern. However, under *nothing* are a number of different patterns that can be sorted out in a second sort. Headers are not provided, but you can create them if you feel they are needed. Warn students to look for oddballs. A second sort of the *nothing* column will look something like the following:

CVVC	CVCC	CV/CVV	oddball
reading	spelling	snowing	fixing
floating	talking	going	
cheering	working		
growling	pushing		

4. Ask, **What do you notice about *going, snowing*, and *fixing*?** Although *snowing* might appear to be a CVC word that requires doubling, the final *w* is part of a vowel pattern rather than a consonant. *Fixing* has the CVC pattern but does not double. This is a rare exception to the rule. Show other words such as *tax*, *box*, or *mix* that do not double because double-*x* is not a pattern that occurs in English, most likely because *x* represents the blend of two letter/sounds: /k/ + /s/.

5. Wrap up the reflection by asking, **What did you learn from this sort? What are the rules about adding -*ing*? What is an exception?** Help students conclude that, in most cases, the -*ing* is simply added to the word and that it is only when a word fits the CVC or CVCe pattern that a change to the base word is needed. Add to or revise the list of rules that you have been generating after each sort.

Extend: When students record this sort in their word study notebooks, ask them to sort both by the rule and by the patterns. You might sort all the words from lessons 2, 3, and 4 by "double, e-drop, or nothing" as a review. Students should look back at word hunts from the previous weeks to find oddball words they can now sort into one of the three categories. (Even words such as *chewing*, *seeing*, *flying*, *studying*, and so on, which have patterns different from the ones included in these sorts, can go under *nothing*.) *Double Scoop* and *Freddy the Hopping, Diving, Jumping Frog* from Chapter 7 in *Words Their Way* are designed to reinforce inflected endings. *Double Scoop* can be downloaded from the PDToolkit.

Apply: It is important that students understand that the rules apply to many more words. Give students additional words and ask them to add -*ing*: *slip, row, sneeze, stir, see, pout, find, mix, do, tap, chew, cheer, love, speed, dress, start, pour, box, draw,* and *win*.

SORT 4   Review of Double, *E*-Drop, and Nothing

double	*e*-drop	nothing	*oddball*
setting	**hiking**	**reading**	
floating	cutting	moving	
stopping	living	spelling	
coming	begging	growling	
grinning	having	cheering	
jogging	sharing	talking	
pushing	humming	working	
fixing	going	snowing	

Sort 5   Adding -*ED* to Words

Generalization: When a base word ends in one vowel and one consonant (CVC), double the consonant before adding -*ed*. If the base words end in a silent *e* (CVCe), drop the *e*. Nothing needs to be done to other base words (CVCC or CVVC).

double	e-drop	nothing	oddball
hopped	hoped	joined	mixed
planned	saved	waited	
grabbed	closed	seemed	
nodded	scored	shouted	
stepped	lived	passed	
dropped	named	wanted	
stirred		acted	
		helped	
		started	
		chewed	

Sorting and Discussion:

1. You might begin this sort by asking your students, **Spell** *hopped* **and** *hoped.* **Did you spell them alike or differently? Why?** See if they can generalize from what they learned from the -*ing* sorts. Explain, **Students often have trouble spelling these words. The sort for this week will help you learn and remember the rules that govern the addition of -***ed***, just as you did for -***ing***.**

2. Students can sort independently, or you can begin with a teacher-directed sort by introducing the headers and key words and modeling your thinking: **Here is the word** *hopped.* **I notice that the** *p* **was doubled before adding -***ed***, so I will put it under "double."** After sorting the key words say, **Help me sort the rest of the words. Think about what happened to the base word.**

3. Begin the reflection by asking, **What do you notice about the words under "double"? What is the pattern in the base words?** (CVC) **What is the pattern under "e-drop"?** (CVCe) **What do you notice about the words under "nothing"?** (There are several patterns: CVVC and CVCC.) **Can you find some oddballs?** (*Fix* is an oddball because it has the CVC pattern, but the *w* in *chew* is part of the vowel, so it is not a CVC word.)

4. Wrap up the reflection by asking, **What did you learn about adding -***ed***?** Help the students see that the rules are similar to the rules for adding -*ing* and can be summed up as "double, *e*-drop, or nothing." Add to the rule chart for this unit. Revisit the question of how to spell *hopping* and *hoping*. Ask about the base word in each and talk about how to spell them based on the rules covered in this sort.

Extend: Talk about the fact that adding -*ed* means that something has already happened and that such words are said to be in the past tense. Model, and then have students create, sentences that include the base word and the past tense: *Don't step in that hole. I stepped in it yesterday and sprained my ankle.* Some sentence frames can get them started: *I want to _____. Yesterday I _____.*

Challenge your students to sort these words in a second sort by the sound of the -*ed* ending, as shown below. English learners may have difficulty doing this, so pair them with native English speakers to assist in pronunciation. This sound sort will help students see that, even when a word sounds like it should be spelled with a *t*, as in WALKT for *walked*, the past tense must be spelled with -*ed*. No headers are provided for this sort, but they are indicated here for clarity. Ask students if they can see any letter patterns in the base words in each column. They might notice that certain consonants precede certain sounds (*p* before /t/, *d* and *t* before /id/) and that the words in the last column have added a syllable to the base word.

/t/	/d/		/id/
hopped	planned	lived	nodded
mixed	grabbed	joined	waited
stepped	closed	seemed	shouted
dropped	scored	stirred	acted
hoped	named	chewed	wanted
passed	saved		started
helped			

Apply: Ask students to apply their knowledge by adding -*ed* to additional words: *march, tame, beg, clean, wave, boil, clip, name, mail, scoop, call, talk, climb, snap, melt, shove, show, thaw, race,* and *pet*. Students could also add -*ing* to these words. Challenge them to write sentences that use all three tenses: *Can you help me? I helped you yesterday and I will probably be helping you tomorrow.*

SORT 5   Adding -*ED* to Words

double	e-drop	nothing	oddball
hopped	**hoped**	**joined**	
acted	planned	saved	
waited	wanted	grabbed	
closed	mixed	helped	
nodded	scored	shouted	
started	stirred	stepped	
named	passed	dropped	
chewed	lived	seemed	

Sort 6   Irregular Verbs

This sort will help students see that not all verbs form the past tense by adding -*ed*. This may be especially helpful for English learners. While some irregular words fall into patterns, most are formed in a variety of ways, so there is no spelling generalization that is useful.

Generalization: Some verbs do not add -*ed*. Instead the past tense is spelled differently.

present	past
sleep	**slept**
keep	kept
slide	slid
shine	shone
freeze	froze
draw	drew
sweep	swept
drive	drove
bleed	bled
know	knew
throw	threw
say	said

Sorting and Discussion:

1. Prepare a set of words to use for teacher-directed modeling. Read over the words together. Explain: **These words are all verbs. They describe things you can do**—*sleep, throw, drive.*
2. Introduce the headers and give some examples of *present* and *past* tense. Remind students, **You have learned to add** -*ed* **to verbs to show that something happened in the past.** Write *hiked, sleeped, slided,* and *knowed.* **Here is an example:** *Last Sunday I hiked 10 miles.* **But does this sound right?** *Last night I hardly sleeped at all. My dad slided into the ditch this morning. I knowed how to ride a bike when I was in first grade.* Then ask, **What is the past tense of** *sleep, slide,* **and** *know*? Write the correct past tense for each.
3. **Can you find pairs of words to sort under present and past tense?** Model with *sleep* and *slept* and then let students complete the sort.

4. **What do you notice about these pairs?** There are different ways to show that something happened in the past. Explain, **These are called irregular verbs because they do not use** -*ed* **for the past tense. Do you see any patterns in the spelling of these pairs?** Challenge your students to come up with a way to sort the pairs of words into categories. Students should describe the categories in their own way and brainstorm additional words that could be added in each one. Following is a possible sort:

vowel change	change to -*ew*	-*eep* to -*ept*	long to short
shine shone	know knew	sleep slept	bleed bled
drive drove	throw threw	keep kept	slide slid
freeze froze	draw drew	sweep swept	

Extend: There are many irregular verbs, but they are not easy to find in a word hunt. Students might set aside a part of their word study notebook to add others over time. For a complete list, check the Internet. Instead of a blind sort, partners can lay one set of words face down and play a game of concentration or memory to find pairs that go together. You might also want to make these games out of sturdier materials to play over time as a way to review these words. Ask students to complete the worksheet on page 27 for additional practice with these verbs. The answer key is below.

1. slept	2. swept	3. drew	4. knew
5. drove	6. froze	7. shone	8. kept
9. threw	10. said		

Apply: Give students the present tense of the following words and ask them to supply the past tense: *feed/fed, meet/met, hide/hid, bite/bit, come/came, eat/ate, teach/taught, bring/brought, think/thought, fight/fought, seek/sought, catch/caught, send/sent, lend/lent, drink/drank, write/wrote, swim/swam, rise/rose, ride/rode, grow/grew, fly/flew, pay/paid, lay/laid.* Suggest that they try the sentence pattern *Yesterday I _____* to help them determine the past tense.

Note: The past tenses of *lay, pay,* and *say* are all formed the same way (*laid, paid, said*), so maybe *said* is not so strange after all!

SORT 6   Irregular Verbs

present	past	
sleep	**slept**	keep
slide	shine	freeze
sweep	bleed	throw
know	threw	drew
knew	bled	swept
froze	draw	shone
say	slid	said
drove	kept	drive

Worksheet for Irregular Verbs

Name_____

Write the past tense for each underlined word in the second sentence.

1. I can't go to <u>sleep</u> this early. I _____ too long last night!

2. It's your turn to <u>sweep</u> up today. I _____ yesterday.

3. What should I <u>draw</u> today? Yesterday I _____ a landscape.

4. I <u>know</u> how to juggle. I _____ how to juggle last year too.

5. Mom can't <u>drive</u> this time. She _____ last time.

6. It might <u>freeze</u> again tonight. Last night, it _____.

7. The sun will <u>shine</u> again today. Yesterday it _____ very brightly.

8. I want to <u>keep</u> this picture. I already _____ two others.

9. Baseball pitchers want to <u>throw</u> strikes. My brother _____ lots of strikes last year!

10. Can you <u>say</u> hello? I already _____ it.

Sort 7 Plural Endings: Adding *-ES*

Not all students will need this sort, but it is a good review. Adding *-es* to a base word adds another syllable. This makes the *-es* ending easy to identify and spell.

Generalization: Words ending in *-ch, -sh, -x,* and *-s* add *-es* instead of just *-s*.

add *-es*				add *-s*	oddball
-ch	*-sh*	*-x*	*-s*		
benches	brushes	foxes	guesses	**chairs**	clothes*
speeches	splashes	mixes	kisses	books	
lunches	crashes	taxes	classes	changes	
churches	ashes			places	
peaches	leashes				
ditches					
branches					
watches					

*High-frequency word

Sorting and Discussion:

1. Write the words: *chairs, changes,* and *benches.* Remind students, **When we want to talk about more than one, we usually add -s to a word to make it plural** (point to *chairs* and *changes*). **Sometimes, however, -es is added** (point to *benches*). **Our sort today will help us learn a rule about when to add -es.**
2. Ask, **How are these words alike?** (They are all plurals or mean more than one.) **Can you find other words that added an -s or -es? Think about the base word!** Sort the words first by the headers. Underlining the base word will help students to see that the *e* is not dropped before *s* as it is before *-ed* and *-ing.*
3. Push the words that simply added *-s* to the side and ask, **What do you notice about the words under -es? Listen as we read them aloud.** Help students see that the *-es* adds another syllable in these words—they can hear it. **Can you find one that does not?** The oddball in this sort is

clothes. Why is it odd? It is not really a plural of *cloth,* but it is a plural. The *-es* does not add another syllable.

4. Sort again using Guess My Category. Put *benches, brushes, foxes,* and *guesses* into separate categories and sort one more word in each category without explaining why. Then hold up the next word and ask if someone knows where it will go. Continue to sort, but do not allow students to explain the categories until the end.
5. Guide the reflection by asking, **How are the words in each column alike? What have we learned about adding -es?** Help students articulate a rule (add *-es* to words that end in *ch, sh, x,* and *s*) and add it to the class chart. Because adding *-es* to make a word plural adds the syllable /*ez*/ to the word, students should have little difficulty spelling the plural form.

Note: Most words ending in *-th* just add *s* (i.e., *paths, truths, months*), but there are a few that add *es* when the *th* is voiced (i.e., *bathes, breathes, soothes,* and *wreathes*). *Clothes* is an oddball in either case.

Extend: Create headers by underlining the final letters in the base word of *ben<u>ch</u>es, bru<u>sh</u>es, fo<u>x</u>es,* and *gue<u>ss</u>es* to guide students when they sort on their own or with a partner. Look for the books *If You Were a Plural Word* by Trisha S. Shaskan and Sara Gray and *Fish and Puppies, Thieves and Guppies* by Brian P. Cleary and Brian Gable. They cover the features in the next two sorts as well.

A word hunt may turn up words that are not plural nouns but are instead present tense, third person, singular verbs (*she relaxes, he stretches, it matches*). These should be accepted. You might ask students to go through the words for this week to identify those that can be both nouns and verbs (*watches, crashes, mixes, changes,* etc.). Help them create sentences that show the word used as both: Many people no longer wear *watches.* Mom *watches* the news every evening.

Apply: Give students transfer words to practice applying the rules: *switch, house, glass, mess, glove, choice, witch, song, flame, pass, match, smash lash, crash, scratch, sketch, box, fix, mess, shape, bunch, grade, wish, drink,* and *mask.*

SORT 7   Plural Endings: Adding -*ES*

add -*es*	add -*s*	*oddball*
benches	**chairs**	foxes
guesses	brushes	speeches
splashes	lunches	clothes
mixes	churches	crashes
books	peaches	classes
kisses	taxes	ditches
leashes	changes	branches
watches	places	ashes

Sort 8   Unusual Plurals

Generalization: Sometimes plurals are formed in unusual ways, such as *mouse* and *mice* or *tooth* and *teeth*. Words that end in *f* sometimes change the *f* to *v* and add -*es*.

f to v + es		vowel change		no change
wife	**wives**	**foot**	**feet**	**sheep**
leaf	leaves	woman*	women	deer
loaf	loaves	mouse	mice	
life	lives	tooth	teeth	
wolf	wolves	goose	geese	
knife	knives			

Sorting and Discussion:

1. Do not show the headers until the very end. Ask, **Do you have any ideas about how we will sort these words?** Or, **What do you notice about these words?** Hopefully, students will notice that there are base words and plurals. Explain, **Let's start by matching the words that go together.** As you start to pair the words, ask, **Which word means only one? Which one means more than one?** Put the singular on the left and the plural on the right. *Sheep* and *deer* will not have a plural match, so talk about how they can mean *1 deer* or *10 deer* or *1 sheep* or *100 sheep*. Set them aside.
2. Continue the sort by asking, **Do you see some pairs that go together because they form the plural the same way?** Pull out the key words *wife* and *wives* and ask, **What happened to the base word *wife* to make it plural?** (The *f* was changed to a *v*.) **Are there more words like**

this? **What do you notice about the words that are left?** Pull out *foot* and *feet*. **What changed in the plural?** (The vowel changed.) **Are there others like this?** Introduce the headers ("*f* to *v* + *es*," "vowel change," and "no change").
3. Ask students, **What did you learn from this sort?** Remind them how they learned that the past tense can be formed in different ways, and in this sort they learned that plurals can be formed in different ways as well. Assure them that there are not a lot of these, but they will need to remember them. Words ending in *f* sometimes change to *v*, so this rule can be added to the class chart. **Note:** This is not always true (e.g., *puffs, cliffs, chiefs*), but sound is a clue because you can hear the /*v*/ sound.

Extend: Have students sort under the headers and arrange pairs together as shown above. Instead of a blind sort, partners might turn one set of words face down and play a game of memory or concentration to find matches. *Sheep* and *deer* can go together as the only ones without a pair. There are few of these unusual plurals, so students will have a hard time finding more in a word hunt, but more examples can be found in the books *If You Were a Plural Word* by Trisha S. Shaskan and Sara Gray and *Fish and Puppies, Thieves and Guppies* by Brian P. Cleary and Brian Gable.

Apply: Students can be asked to write the plural of *half, cliff, hoof, calf, puff, shelf, elf, thief,* and *chief.* Warn them to listen for a difference in sound between words like *cliffs* and *calves.* Ask them about the plural of *man* (*men*), *fish,* and *child* (*children*) by using the sentence: *I saw one _____ and then I saw two _____.*

SORT 8   Unusual Plurals

f to *v* + *es*	vowel change	no change
wife	wives	sheep
foot	feet	loaf
lives	women	leaves
leaf	geese	woman
mouse	loaves	life
wolves	mice	goose
knives	knife	wolf
tooth	deer	teeth

Sort 9   *Y* + Inflected Endings

Generalization: When a base word ends in a consonant and a *y*, change the *y* to *i* before adding *-es* and *-ed*.

base word	+ -s	+ -ed	+ -ing
play	plays	played	playing
stay	stays	stayed	staying
spray	sprays	sprayed	spraying
fry	fries	fried	frying
cry	cries	cried	crying
spy	spies	spied	spying

Sorting and Discussion:

1. Students should be able to sort these words independently using the headers, but warn them to look for a new rule when adding the endings. For a teacher-directed sort, introduce the headers and say, **Let's find the base words first and then we'll match the words that have the same base.**

2. After sorting independently or as a group say, **Let's look at the base words. Do you see two different patterns? What are they?** (Words ending in *-y* and *–ay*.) Arrange all the words with the same base word together if you have not already done so, separating those that end in *-ay* and *-y*. Ask, **What happened to base words ending in *-y*? When does the *y* change to an *i*?** (Before *-ed* and *-es*.) **Why doesn't the *y* change to an *i* before adding *-ing*?** (Double *i* seldom occurs in English! *Skiing* is an exception.)

3. Help students reach a conclusion by asking, **What did you learn about adding *-es* and *-ed* to base words ending in *-y*?** Be sure you talk about changing the *y* to *i* only when the *y* comes after a consonant. Help students articulate a rule and add it to the chart you have been keeping throughout this unit.

Extend: This sort does not work very well as a blind sort with a partner. Instead, assign students to select a base word from each category (with *-ay* and *-y*) and write sentences using the words with endings added. A word hunt may not be very productive, but some two-syllable words might turn up (*bunnies*,

carried). Challenge students to write the base words for each one.

Apply: Give students words to apply the generalization. Ask them to add *-ing*, *-ed*, and *-es/-s* to *dry*, *stray*, *fly*, *carry*, and *sway*. The word *fly* offers a special challenge because the past tense is *flew*. Ask the students to write the plurals of *puppy*, *valley*, *party*, *monkey*, *berry*, and *birthday*.

UNIT REVIEW AND ASSESSMENT

Review:

After many sorts that focus on base words and inflected endings, your chart of rules may look quite complicated. Now is the time to review and simplify it. The following list covers most cases, and these rules are really the only ones students need to remember for now.

> **Double.** When a word ends in one vowel and one consonant, you double the consonant before adding *-ed* and *-ing*. (**Note:** This is sometimes called the *One, One, One Rule*: 1 vowel, 1 consonant, 1 syllable: double.)
>
> *e*-**Drop.** When a word ends in silent *e*, you drop the *e* before adding *-ing* and *-ed*.
>
> **Change *y* to *i*.** When a word ends in a consonant and a *y*, you change the *y* to *i* before adding *-ed* or *-es*.
>
> **Add *-es*.** When words end in *s*, *sh*, *ch*, or *x*, add *-es*. For words ending in *f*, you sometimes change the *f* to *v* and add *-es*.
>
> **Nothing.** Otherwise, just do nothing and add the ending.

Students can review all these rules by sorting words from previous sorts into these five categories. (Omit the irregular verbs and plurals.) This is a good time to play games that will reinforce these rules, such as *Double Scoop* and *Freddy the Hopping, Diving, Jumping Frog*, described in *Words Their Way*. Adapt these games to review all the rules.

Assess:

Use Unit Spell Check 1B on page 13 as a posttest to assess student mastery of the rules in this unit.

SORT 9   *Y* + Inflected Endings

base word	+-s	+-ed	+-ing
play	fry	stays	
crying	plays	fried	
sprays	fries	played	
playing	frying	spies	
staying	sprayed	cries	
spraying	cry	spied	
spy	stay	stayed	
cried	spray	spying	

Unit II   Compound Words

NOTES FOR THE TEACHER

Background and Objectives

Compound words show up early in children's reading, and teachers talk about such words when they arise. Spelling compound words is not especially challenging *if* students know how to spell the two words that make up the compound word. For this reason, we place the formal study of compound words here in the early syllables and affixes stage, when students have learned the patterns in one-syllable words. We want to introduce the idea that there are familiar words (morphemic units) within longer words that make those words easier to understand, read, and spell—some of the key understandings of this stage. Students will be able to:

- Identify and define compound words as words that are made up of two other words
- Spell the words in these sorts

We offer three sorts here in this short unit. The first two use words that are concrete and easy to define, while Sort 12 has more abstract but commonly used words. This should be enough to introduce the term *compound words* and to get your students attuned to looking for them in the reading and writing they do all the time. No spell check is included for this unit.

Targeted Learners

These sorts are optional and can be used anytime. Students in the early syllables and affixes stage should already be able to spell the two words that make up the compound word and can explore the meanings of the words. These sorts might be especially helpful to English learners who will benefit from the attention paid to word meanings. Not all languages create words by compounding, so some explicit instruction with this feature of English is important.

Teaching Tips

Use the same weekly routines described on pages 6–8 with some modifications. Rather than hunting for words that fit the specific categories established with the words in the sort (e.g., more words with *light*), word hunts can focus on finding any compound words.

Give students one word (for example, *man*) and challenge them to think of as many compound words as possible (*manmade, manhole, manhandle,* etc.). *Brainburst*, described in Chapter 8 of the core text *Words Their Way*, can make the brainstorming described above into a game using these suggested words: *man, air, back, eye, hand, foot, home, horse, house, land, life, night, out, over, play, road, sand, sea, under, water,* and *wind*.

Students often enjoy illustrating the meaning of both the words that make up the compound words as well as the final word (*snow + man = snowman*). Ask your students to pick five words and draw a picture that will make the meaning of each clear. Older students often enjoy illustrating more abstract compound words, such as those in Sort 12. For example, *checkout, outside,* and *sideways* offer creative possibilities. Such drawings might be displayed or collected into a class book. You might also create a version of *Homophone Win, Lose, or Draw,* described in Chapter 6 of *Words Their Way,* that features compound words.

Students can set aside a section of their word study notebooks to record more compound words they find over time, or the class might create a bulletin board or chart that they add to during the entire year. Hyphenated words might be added as well because these are often confused with compound words. (Is it *goodbye* or *good-bye*?) A list of compound words can be found in the Word List Appendix of *Words Their Way,* and many more lists can be found on the Internet. Finding words in reading materials, however, will be more meaningful than giving students lists.

Literature Connection

Share books about compound words: *Thumbtacks, Earwax, Lipstick, Dipstick: What Is a Compound Word?* by Brian P. Cleary and Brian Gable, and *If You Were a Compound Word* by Trisha Speed Shaskan and Sara Gray.

Sort 10   Compound Words

Generalization: Compound words are made up of two words joined together. Each word contributes to the meaning of the longer word.

bookcase	lighthouse	downhill
bookmark	lightweight	downstairs
notebook	daylight	downtown
cookbook	flashlight	downpour
scrapbook	sunlight	countdown
	(headlight)	

headache	snowman
headfirst	snowflake
(headlight)	snowstorm
headphones	snowplow
headstrong	

Sorting and Discussion:

1. Show your students all the words without going over the meanings in advance (that will come later). Ask, **What do you notice about all these words?** Take various responses, but be sure to talk about how the words are all made up of two words. Introduce or review the term *compound words* and define with examples: **Compound words are made of two words:** *bookcase*, **for example, is made up of** *book* **and** *case*.

2. **Do you have any ideas about how to sort these words?** Students should quickly spot the common elements, but if they do not, be ready to model a category to get started. Note that the word *headlight* can be sorted in two different places. Set up the bolded key words as headers and then sort the rest of the words with student help.

3. After sorting, read down the words in each column and ask, **How are the words in this column alike?** Then say, **Let's talk about the meaning of each compound word and how it is related to the two words that make it up. For example, a bookmark marks your place in a book; sunlight is the light that comes from the sun.** Some compound words cannot be interpreted so literally. *Headstrong* does not literally mean "strong in the head" but rather "strong willed." Ask students to look up the meaning of a few words such as this one as part of the group discussion.

4. Have students repeat the sort under your supervision. Ask them to identify the parts of words that might be hard to spell, such as the *ache* in *headache* or the *weight* in *lightweight*. Reflect by asking, **What did you learn from this sort? What is a compound word?**

Extend: Have students complete standard weekly routines described on pages 6–8. During a word hunt, have them look for any compound word and consider creating a chart or setting aside a section in their word study notebook where more can be added over time.

Have students brainstorm other words that share these same word parts. Some examples include: *bookkeeper, bookworm, textbook, downstream, download, downcast, downfall, headband, headway, headline, snowfall, snowdrift, snowshoe,* and *snowball.* Call at least 10 words aloud for students to spell for a weekly assessment.

Apply: Give students these word parts and ask them to create compound words: *boat, cut, bow, base, cow, ball, hair, boy, rain, row.*

SORT 10   Compound Words

bookcase	**light**house	**snow**man
headache	**down**hill	headphones
downstairs	headfirst	bookmark
snowflake	downtown	daylight
flashlight	notebook	downpour
snowstorm	headlight	cookbook
scrapbook	sunlight	countdown
snowplow	headstrong	lightweight

Sort 11   More Compound Words

If you have done Sort 10, you can assign this sort to be done independently.

Generalization: Compound words are made up of two words joined together that are related to the meaning of the longer word.

backpack	homework	driveway
background	homesick	hallway
backyard	homemade	stairway
backbone	hometown	wayside
backtrack	homestretch	doorway
backfire		
lifeboat	earache	
lifelike	earring	
lifeguard	eardrum	
lifelong	earplug	

Sorting and Discussion:

1. Show your students all the words without going over the meanings in advance (that will come later). Ask, **What do you notice about all these words?** Take various responses, but be sure to talk about how the words are all made up of two words. Introduce or review the term *compound words* and define with examples: **Compound words are composed of two words, such as *backpack*, which is made up of *back* and *pack*.**
2. **Do you have any ideas about how to sort these words?** Students should quickly spot the common elements, but if they do not, be ready to model a category to get started. Students can sort independently or together.
3. After sorting, read down the words in each column and identify the common element. Then say, **Let's talk about the meaning of each compound word and how it is related to the two words that make it up. For example, homework is school work you do at home.** Some compound words cannot be interpreted so literally. *Backbone* usually refers to "character" rather than a "spine." *Backfire* is used to refer to an unexpected and unwanted effect. Ask students to look up the meaning of a few words as part of the group discussion.
4. Reflect by asking, **What did you learn from this sort? What is a compound word? How does the meaning of each word contribute to the meaning of the compound? Is this always clear?**

Extend: Complete standard weekly routines described on pages 6–8. During a word hunt, have students look for any compound word to add to a chart or section in their word study notebook. Have students brainstorm other words that share these same word parts. Some examples include: *bareback, backfield, backhand, backlash, backrest, homebody, downhome, homespun, freeway, lifeline, afterlife, waylaid, earphone,* and *earshot*. Call at least 10 words aloud for students to spell for a weekly assessment.

Apply: You might give students these word parts and ask them to create compound words: *foot, road, walk, tip, bare, ball, side, base, day, fish, birth, gold, toe, rail.*

SORT 11   More Compound Words

backpack	**home**work	drive**way**
lifeboat	**ear**ache	background
earring	homesick	homestretch
hallway	backyard	stairway
earplug	wayside	lifeguard
lifelong	homemade	backbone
backtrack	lifelike	hometown
doorway	backfire	eardrum

Sort 12 Abstract Compound Words

If you have done Sorts 10 and 11, you can assign this sort to be done independently.

Generalization: Compound words are made up of two words joined together. Sometimes they are not easily defined by the two words that make them up.

somebody	himself	anyone
(something)	themselves	everyone
sometime	yourself	(someone)
somewhere	herself	
somehow	myself*	
(someone)	itself	
everything	**without**	**inside**
anything*	outside	beside
nothing	throughout	sideways
(something)	checkout	

*High-frequency word

Sorting and Discussion:

1. Show your students all the words and ask, **What do you notice about all these words?** Review the term *compound words*. Students should be able to sort independently using the bolded key words as headers. Some words can go in more than one category, as shown by those in parentheses.

2. After sorting, read down the words in each column and identify the common element. Explain, **These words are compound words that you will often see and hear, but they are not easy to define. Let's use some in a sentence.** For example, *I walked beside the road.*

3. Point out the plural of *self* in *themselves* to review how the *f* changes to a *v* before adding -es.

Extend: Assign standard routines. Have students think of other words that share these same word parts. Some examples include: *someday, plaything, blackout, blowout, cookout, hideout, outfit, checkout, timeout, outfield, outlaw, outlast, outline, outlive, everywhere, everyplace,* and *hillside.* Ask students to look for any compound words they can find when doing a word hunt rather than looking for more words with these same word parts. Call at least 10 words aloud to be spelled for a weekly test.

Review compound words by playing *Brainburst* using *man, air, back, hand, foot, horse, house, land, life, night, out, over, play, road, sand, sea, under, water,* and *wind.* Give teams of students one word at a time to think of as many compound words as they can. Teams then share their words, but only unique words that no other team thought of can earn a point. See details in Chapter 8 of *Words Their Way.*

Apply: Ask students to use five of the words from the sort in sentences.

SORT 12   Abstract Compound Words

s<u>ome</u>body	**him<u>self</u>**	**every<u>thing</u>**
any<u>one</u>	**with<u>out</u>**	**in<u>side</u>**
something	itself	everyone
outside	anything	beside
sometime	yourself	throughout
sideways	herself	somewhere
nothing	somehow	someone
myself	checkout	themselves

Unit III Syllable Juncture

NOTES FOR THE TEACHER

Background and Objectives

Syllable juncture is a term used to describe the point at which two syllables join. The pattern of vowels and consonants that meet at this point sends cues to the reader about the likely point of division that might be useful in decoding an unfamiliar word and the sound of the vowel in the first syllable. Learning about the patterns of vowels and consonants on either side of the syllable juncture helps spellers, too. For example, spellers face decisions such as whether to put one or two consonants in the middle of a word (e.g., is it *dinner* or *diner*?). Knowledge of syllable juncture patterns is therefore a useful tool for analyzing the longer words that readers and spellers encounter.

In referring to **syllable juncture patterns**, the focus is on the middle of the word where a *V* stands for a vowel letter and a *C* for a consonant letter. There may be one or more consonants on either side (VCV = *tulip*, *silent*, and *flavor*), but these usually do not affect the spelling or sound of the vowel at the juncture. The patterns that are covered in this unit include open and closed syllables and their variations: VCV, VCCV, VCCCV, VVCV, and VV. The other syllable patterns will be covered in the study of vowel patterns in stressed syllables that follows in Unit IV. The most reliable pattern of vowels and consonants is the VCCV pattern in words such as *les-son* and *nap-kin*. The VCCV pattern regularly signals that the first syllable is **closed** with a short-vowel sound (i.e., *les* and *nap*). A variation of the VCCV pattern is the closed VCCCV pattern as in *pil-grim*.

The VCV pattern most often represents the **open** syllable with a long-vowel sound in the first syllable, as in *su-per* and *di-ner*, when the syllable is split after the long vowel (V/CV) and left "open" (e.g., *su* and *di*). However, there are also words in which the syllable division comes after the consonant (VC/V),

as in *wag-on*, where the first syllable (*wag*) is closed and has a short-vowel sound. It is important to note, though, that the V/CV open pattern occurs over two-thirds of the time in two-syllable words. Variations of the open-syllable pattern are the VVCV pattern in *reason* and the VV pattern in *create*. We suggest you introduce and use the terms *open* and *closed* when referring to syllables.

Many teachers find these sorts to be some of the most challenging to do with their students because they themselves may be unfamiliar with the features and terms. You undoubtedly have intuitive knowledge about syllables, but you will learn along with your students as that knowledge is made explicit through these sorts. Students will:

- Identify the pattern where syllables join (VCV, VCCV, VV, etc.)
- Identify the vowel sound in the first syllable
- Separate words into syllables using open and closed syllables as guides
- Spell the words in these sorts correctly

Targeted Learners

These sorts are designed for students in the middle syllables and affixes stage who make errors at the point where syllables join. They may spell BOTLE for *bottle* or FAVVOR for *favor*, using but confusing the number of letters in the middle of two-syllable words. Use Unit Spell Check 3 on page 46 to determine more exactly whether students need these sorts.

Teaching Tips

The words selected for this unit are among the most frequent two-syllable words and should be easy to read and understand by most students in the middle syllables and affixes stage. The words in Sort 16 are not as common, but this is a logical place to introduce and contrast the patterns. More words are suggested in the lists that follow most sorts and in the appendix to *Words Their Way*. You might use these lists to develop more sorts and sorts with more challenging words, or you might ask students to apply what they have learned in the word sorts to read and spell these additional words.

Remember, generalizations are stated for each sort as a guide for teachers. Do *not* begin a lesson by stating the generalization! Instead, use the sort and suggested questions to guide the discussion so that students are able to tell you the generalization in their own words. Telling is not teaching.

Students should work with the words in these sorts using the standard weekly routines described on pages 6–8. During a word hunt, students should be able to find more words that fit the feature in just about any materials they are reading. The exceptions are the patterns in Sort 16, which are not as common.

Throughout this unit, students will be thinking about how words are broken into syllables. They can be asked to indicate syllable division in their word study notebooks as they write the words (e.g., *su-per* or *su/per*). Do not make too much of an issue, however, about where syllable breaks come in words, and do not send students to the dictionary to resolve disputes: They may find differences in the entry word and the pronunciation key as in *pup pet* and *pup it*. Breaking words into syllables at logical points is a useful tool when new words are encountered or when a word is parsed for spelling, but exact splitting into syllables is not necessary.

As we noted in the Overview, you may wish to use the term *syllable types* as you guide students' examination of the spelling of two-syllable words. In this unit, we address two of the six syllable types: the closed syllable (the syllable is "closed" with a consonant, usually though not always indicating a short-vowel sound) and the open syllable (the syllable is "open" because it ends with a long vowel).

With word processing taking the place of typing, there is less reason to teach students about how to hyphenate words at the end of lines, but this is one more reason to learn about syllable breaks. Look for text to show students (newspapers with their short lines are a good source of examples) in which long words have been hyphenated and point out that words are divided at syllable breaks or before and after an affix. Explain that they might need to hyphenate words in their own writing at times and model how this is done.

The card game *Match* described in Chapter 5 of *Words Their Way* and the *Classic Card Game* and *Word*

Study Uno in Chapter 6 are games that can be adapted for syllable patterns. Card games are popular with students in the middle elementary grades, and any game that has four to five categories can be adapted to review these syllable features.

While the most common words have been chosen for these sorts, there may be many that are unfamiliar to English learners. Because the focus is on the patterns, a full knowledge of all words is not essential when students start a sort, but choose a few words to introduce and ask English learners to think of related words, including cognates in their primary languages. Create a chart of the words with examples that students share, and refer back to it often. Start the sort with the most familiar words. Students will learn pronunciations as they work in small groups and with classmates, but read the words in lists several times for extra support.

Double letters in syllable junctures (*button, lesson*) or at the point where a prefix joins a base word or root (*misspell, illustrate*) are very common in English but not in many other languages. Compare the spelling of these cognates in English and Spanish: *possible/posible, necessary/necesario, occupant/ocupante*. In Spanish, double letters such as *rr* or *ll* signal a different pronunciation (as in *quesadilla*, where the double *l* has the /y/ sound).

UNIT SPELL CHECK 3 ASSESSMENT FOR SYLLABLE JUNCTURE PATTERNS

For a pretest, simply call the 20 words aloud for students to spell as in a traditional spelling test format. Say each word once, use it in a sentence if you feel it is necessary, then say it again. All of these words appear in the sorts.

1. summer	**2.** easy	**3.** finish
4. poet	**5.** leader	**6.** lion
7. river	**8.** hundred	**9.** never
10. complete	**11.** reason	**12.** English
13. giant	**14.** lazy	**15.** saving
16. tiger	**17.** moment	**18.** number
19. sister	**20.** waited	

For the posttest, you can assess in the same way, or you may want to photocopy and enlarge page 46. Say each word clearly and ask your students to write the word in the box labeled with the correct vowel pattern, as shown below. Tell them to think about the letters in the middle of the words as you call them aloud. Then write each word under the heading that shows the pattern of letters in the middle. Allow time for students to check their work and reorganize their words if needed. The reproducible form can be found on the next page.

VCCV	VCCCV	VC/V first syllable short
summer	English	river
number	hundred	finish
sister	complete	never

V/CV first syllable long	VVCV	VV
tiger	reason	lion
moment	easy	giant
lazy	leader	poet
saving	waited	

Interpreting Scores on Pre- and Posttests

Use the goal-setting form on page 4 to analyze and record results, and use the pacing guide on page 5 to plan which sorts to use.

- **90% or better**—Students can move on to the next unit, but you might use Sort 17 to review open and closed syllables and how they are related to the addition of inflected endings.
- **75% to 85%**—A "gray area" where teacher judgment is needed. Students may need only some sorts. Examine the types of errors students make to see if there are particular features that can be targeted rather than doing all the sorts. You might skip Sort 13.
- **70% or less**—Students will benefit from doing all the sorts in the unit. Be sure, however, that they have an adequate score on vowel patterns in the within word pattern stage.

Unit Spell Check 3   Assessment for Syllable Juncture Patterns

Name _____

Directions: Listen to the word your teacher calls aloud. Think of the letters in the middle of the word. Write the word under the heading that shows the pattern of letters.

1. VCCV	2. VCCCV	3. VC/V first syllable short
_____ _____ _____	_____ _____ _____	_____ _____ _____

4. V/CV first syllable long	5. VVCV	6. VV
_____ _____ _____	_____ _____ _____	_____ _____ _____

Sort 13 Syllable Juncture in VCV and VCCV Patterns

Students will be looking at a completely different feature of words and learning new terms, so we recommend that you start with a teacher-directed sort. Allow some extra time for this sort, or extend the discussion over two days.

Generalization: An open syllable that ends in a vowel usually has a long-vowel sound. A closed syllable that ends in a consonant usually has a short-vowel sound. Double letters in the middle of a word signal a short vowel in the first syllable.

VCV	VCCV	oddball
super	**supper**	busy
diner	dinner	
tiger	happy*	
later	pretty*	
paper	penny	
zero	puppy	
over*	rabbit	
unit	kitten	
crazy	hello	
open*	letter	
tiny	lesson	
	summer	

*High-frequency word

Explore Meaning: Students will probably know the meaning of the words in this sort, but find out what they associate with *dinner* and *supper*. Are they the same? Most would probably agree that a supper comes in the evening, while dinner can come either at noon or in the evening and is more formal.

Sorting and Discussion:

1. Prepare a set of words for sorting on a table, whiteboard, or pocket chart. Set a purpose for sorting by asking your students: **Spell *super*, *supper*, *diner*, and *dinner*. Why did you spell them that way?** Accept their ideas, but do not give away any right answers at this point. Explain, **The sort you are doing this week will help you understand what is going on with words like these.**

2. Show students the words in the sort and ask, **What do you notice about these words?** Take a number of responses, but be sure to talk about how the words have two syllables and that some have double consonants in the middle. Then say, **This week you will be looking at patterns in a different way.** Introduce the headers VCV and VCCV, and put the key words *super* and *supper* under the headers. Explain, **The letters in the headers refer only to the pattern of vowels and consonants in the middle of the word where two syllables come together.** Underline the letters in the words and label them: **VCV represents the *u*, *p*, and *e* in *super*, whereas VCCV represents the *u*, *p*, *p*, and *e* in *supper*. One or more letters, or no letters, can come on either side of the pattern in the middle.**

3. Sort the words *diner* and *dinner*, and briefly talk about what they mean. Begin to involve your students in the sorting process by saying, **Help me sort the rest of these words.** Continue, with your students' help, to sort under each header. For now, the oddball *busy*, which has the pattern but not the long sound of *u*, should be sorted under VCV.

4. Next, read down the VCV column of words, emphasizing the syllables and then say, **What do you notice about all of these words?** Demonstrate how to break words into two syllables by cutting them apart or by drawing a line between the two syllables, as in *su/per*. **What do you notice about the vowel sound in the first syllable of each word?** Students should notice that in each word, the vowel sound is long except for the word *busy*. Move this word to the oddball category. Then explain, **Syllables that end with a long-vowel sound are called "open." You have studied open syllables in words that end with a vowel, such as *go*, *row*, and *blue*.** You can write the word *open* over the VCV pattern letters. You might point out or model how your mouth is left open after saying the vowel.

5. Next, read down the VCCV column, emphasizing the syllables. **What do you notice about all of these words?** Again cut apart the words or draw a line between the syllables (*sup/per*) and explain, **What do you notice about the vowel sound in the first syllable of each word? These syllables are called "closed" because the short-vowel sound is followed by a consonant. Words such as *fled*, *drag*, *trip*, and *stop* end with a consonant and have short vowels.** You can write the word *closed* over the VCV pattern letters. You might point out or model how parts of your mouth often close to articulate the consonant at the end of the syllable: *sum-mer*, *sup-per*, *pen-ny*.

6. Have students sort their own words under your supervision using the headers, and ask them to check their sort by reading down each column listening for the vowel sound. *Zero* can be pronounced with either a long *e* in the first syllable /ze-ro/ or an *r*-influenced vowel /zir-o/ depending on the dictionary.

7. Begin the reflection by asking, **What did you learn about two-syllable words in this sort?** Probe with other questions as needed to help students reach a conclusion. **When is the vowel long in the first syllable? When is it short? When is a syllable open? Closed? What can we say now about the spelling of** *super* **and** *supper*? **Why are there two** *p*'s **in** *supper*? (The extra consonant is needed to keep the vowel short.) **Why is** *busy* **an oddball?** Help students articulate a generalization. Record the generalization on a chart to which you and the students can add information as more syllable patterns are covered.

Extend: Students should work with the words using the weekly routines described on pages 6–8. To reinforce the idea of the syllables, ask students to draw a line between them on the word cards or in their word study notebooks. A word hunt will turn up many words as well as oddballs that will foreshadow other sorts to come. Have them put oddballs into a third column and keep them handy for future reference. For a weekly assessment, call aloud at least 10 words from the sort for students to spell.

Because students have not yet studied the final unaccented syllable in words like *bunny* and *letter*, you should draw attention to words that end in *y* and *er* and the sound that is represented. An alternative sort could be by final letters: *-y, -r,* and *-n.* (Unaccented syllables will be studied in more depth in Unit VI. In the meantime, working with the words in weekly routines will help students learn and remember the spellings of the unaccented syllables.)

Apply: Choose some words from the list of additional words below to read and spell. Review the generalization and how it applies to each word: **Spell the word** *muffin*. **Do you double the** *f*? **Why? Spell the word** *humid*. **Do you double the** *m*? **Why not? How do you read this word:** *fellow*? **Is it** *fe-low* **or** *fel-low*? **How can you tell?**

Additional Words: *baby, bonus, basic, humid, tulip, pirate, robot, rodent, unit, hero, blizzard, fellow, hammer, mammal, muffin, puppet, sudden, slipper, tennis, guppy.*

SORT 13   Syllable Juncture in VCV and VCCV Patterns

VCV	VCCV	*oddball*
super	**supper**	diner
dinner	tiger	happy
later	busy	pretty
paper	penny	zero
tiny	over	puppy
rabbit	unit	kitten
hello	crazy	letter
lesson	summer	open

Sort 14   More Syllable Juncture in VCV and VCCV Patterns

Generalization: The short-vowel sound comes before two consonants in the middle of a two-syllable word. The letters may be the same or different. When the first syllable is open in a VCV word, it has the long-vowel sound.

VCV	VCCV doublet	VCCV different	oddball
silent	**happen**	**number***	never*
female	better*	winter	only*
duty	follow	problem	
moment	funny*	after*	
	yellow*	finger	
	pattern	sister*	
	bottom	chapter	
	pillow	member	
		blanket	
		window	

Sorting and Discussion:

1. Quickly read through the words in this sort without showing the pattern headers. Most words should be familiar. If students have completed the previous sort, then they should be ready to respond with many ideas to the question, **What do you notice about these words?** Be sure to talk about how they all have two syllables. Probe for ideas from the previous sort. **What pattern do you see in the middle of these words? What do you notice about the vowel sounds in the first syllable?**

2. Ask students, **Who has an idea about how to sort these words?** Students might be able to sort independently or use a teacher-led Guess My Category Sort. Set up the key words *silent*, *happen*, and *number* as headers. (Keep pattern headers for later.) Sort one more word under each header without explanation. Then hold up another word like *female* and ask, **Where will this word go?** Continue to sort all the words with student help before talking about the reason for the placements. If oddballs are not identified, leave them for now.

3. After sorting, read down each column and emphasize the first syllable. Ask, **What is the same about all the words in this column?** Talk about the vowel sound and the consonants in the middle, and introduce the pattern headers: VCV, VCCV doublet, and VCCV different. Review the terms *open* and *closed*. **Which of these patterns is closed with a consonant? Which one is open ending in a vowel? What are the oddballs and why?** (*Never* has the VCV pattern but has a short vowel, *only* has the VCCV pattern but a long vowel.)

4. Wrap things up by reminding students of the generalization from last week and add to it. **We learned that vowels are long before a single consonant and short before a double consonant. What can we add to that?** (The consonant letters do not have to be the same.) Break apart some of the words under *number* to show the syllables: *num-ber, win-ter, prob-lem*. Ask, **How can this help you as a reader when you come across new words like this?** Dividing words between two consonants can help you figure it out.

Extend: Assign the standard routines from pages 6–8 to complete over the week. Students might go back to the word hunt from the last sort to find words that fit in this new category. Explain that they will be learning more patterns in the middle of words so that eventually they will have a category for more of them. Call aloud at least 10 words for a weekly spell check.

Apply: Choose some words from the list below to read and spell. Review the generalization and how it applies to each word: **Spell the word *basket*. Do you double any letters? Why not?** (There are already two consonants to close the syllable and keep the vowel short.) **Spell the word *crater*. Do you double the *t*?** (No.) **Why not?** (The first syllable ends with a long vowel and is open.) **How do you read this word: *trumpet*. Where would you divide the word into parts?** (*trum-pet*)

Additional Words: *crater, crisis, fever, navy, siren, vacant, blossom, dipper, gallop, butter, matter, hollow, tunnel, valley, basket, center, cactus, dentist, goblet, helmet, insect, kidnap, magnet, master, seldom, tablet, temper, trumpet, basket, wonder.*

SORT 14   More Syllable Juncture in VCV and VCCV Patterns

VCV	VCCV doublet	VCCV different	*oddball*
silent	**happen**	**number**	
funny	winter	follow	
female	better	problem	
after	moment	pattern	
sister	finger	bottom	
chapter	duty	member	
blanket	pillow	never	
only	yellow	window	

Sort 15   Syllable Juncture in VCV and VVCV Patterns

The VCV pattern is most often the open syllable with a long-vowel sound as in *hu-man* (about 75% of the time), but there are also many words in which VCV has a closed syllable, as in *sev-en*. The VVCV juncture pattern is a variation of the open-syllable pattern because the syllable still ends with a vowel that has the long-vowel sound.

Generalization: The first vowel is usually long in the VCV pattern but sometimes it can be short. The first vowel is long in the VVCV pattern.

V/CV (long)	VC/V (short)	VVCV (long)
human	**seven***	**reason**
pilot	river	meeting
student	visit	peanut
humor	wagon	eager
lazy	planet	leader
music	lemon	sneaker
	finish	easy
	limit	
	present	
	second	
	minute	

Explore Meaning: *Present* and *minute* are homographs because they have two pronunciations and meaning. Write the sentence, *Will you present the present to the visitor?* Read it with the students and talk about the pronunciation and meanings. Display the word *minute* and ask students to read and define it. They will most readily identify *minute* as a unit of time and are probably not familiar with the adjective. Introduce the additional pronunciation and meaning ("tiny" as in "a minute amount of salt").

Sorting and Discussion:

1. Without showing the pattern headers, read over the words quickly to be sure students can identify them. These are common words, so they should be familiar to most. Ask, **What do you notice about these words? Do they have a pattern in the middle that we have seen before? Do you see a new pattern in any? What do you notice about the vowels? Any ideas about how we might sort these words?**

2. Set up the key words *human*, *seven*, and *reason*. Sort another word in each category and then proceed as in a Guess My Category Sort. Ask, **Who can tell me where the next word goes?** Agree as a group to put the word *present* under *never* with a short vowel in the first syllable.

3. After sorting, read down each column, emphasizing the first syllable and checking the vowel sounds. Then ask about each category, **What do you notice about the words in each column? What is the vowel sound? What is the pattern in the middle?** Introduce the pattern headers and ask, **Which patterns are open?** (The vowel pair in VVCV is long, so it is also open.) **Which one is closed?** Speculate about why the letter *v* might not be doubled in words such as *seven* and *river*. Write these words with a double *v* and notice how the two *v*s begin to look like a *w*. The letter *v* doesn't double (the rare words *savvy* and *revved* are exceptions).

4. Help students add to the generalizations they have been learning about patterns in the middle of words. **What did you learn from this sort to add to what you know about syllable patterns? How can that help you as a reader and speller?** Write the sentences, *I'd like to present you with a prize* and *The minute dust particles covered the table*, and talk about how a reader needs to be ready to change the vowel when it does not make sense.

Extend: Complete standard weekly routines with these words. In a word hunt, students should look for words with these patterns, but also ask them to revisit earlier word hunts for oddballs that might fit the new categories established here. Review the word hunts and ask, **Which VCV pattern did you find the most often?** They are likely to find more that have a long vowel in the first syllable. Call aloud at least 10 words for students to spell for a weekly assessment.

Help students identify which words in the sort have base words with a suffix added (*meeting*, *sneaker*, *leader*). Point out that examining words for bases and suffixes also helps them decode and remember the spellings of many words. (Unit VIII examines affixes—prefixes and suffixes—in more depth as they combine with different types of base words.)

Apply: Select some less familiar VCV words from below to prepare a list for students to read. Have them practice a flexible decoding strategy, using both a short vowel and a long vowel, to read the word. (Is the word *lab-or* or *la-bor*?) They should check the pronunciation against what makes sense or whether they have heard the word before. Ask students to spell a word like *comet* or *credit*. What makes these words hard to spell? You don't know whether to double the consonant in the middle—is it *commet* or *creddit*? Writing the word and checking to see if it looks right can help. Ask them to spell *liver*. Does the *v* double? (No, it would look like a *w* as in *liwer*.)

Additional Words: *famous, labor, legal, private, recent, spiral, ozone, stupid, chapel, city, comet, credit, critic, denim, dozen, devil, liver, limit, lizard, melon, panel, prison, wizard, waiter, season, eagle, diary, raisin, traitor, beaver.*

SORT 15   Syllable Juncture in VCV and VVCV Patterns

V/CV long	VC/V short	VVCV long
human	**seven**	**reason**
river	pilot	visit
meeting	wagon	planet
lemon	eager	peanut
finish	student	limit
leader	lazy	present
easy	second	music
sneaker	humor	minute

Sort 16   Syllable Juncture in VCCCV and VV Patterns

Generalization: When three consonants come in the middle of a word (VCCCV), look for a blend or digraph as a guide to where the syllables are split (VCC/CV or VC/CCV). Two vowels sometimes represent two syllables (V/V).

VCC/CV	VC/CCV	V/V
athlete	pilgrim	create
kingdom	complete	poet
pumpkin	monster	riot
halfway	kitchen	duet
English	control	trial
mushroom	hundred	cruel*
	inspect	diet
	children	lion†
		poem*
		giant

†May be pronounced as one syllable

Sorting and Discussion:

1. Quickly read through the words in this sort and talk about any that might be unfamiliar. Then ask, **What do you notice about these words?** Show the key word *athlete* and say each syllable: *ath-lete*. Ask, **What is the pattern in the middle?** (VCCCV) **Where do we break it into syllables?** Draw a line to show the syllable break after *th*. Repeat with *pil-grim* and *cre-ate*.
2. Ask, **How should we sort these words?** Using the key words, sort with student help, breaking the words orally between the syllables. You and your students may pronounce words such as *lion, poem,* and *cruel* as one-syllable words. These can be set aside as oddballs.
3. After sorting, read down each column, emphasizing the syllables. Ask, **What is the same about all the words in this column? What do you notice about the words with three consonants in the middle?** (There is always a blend or digraph to show where to split the word.) Introduce the pattern headers. **Which syllables are closed?** (VCC/CV and VC/CCV) **Which are open?** (V/V)

4. Ask students to sort and check their own words if time allows. Then help them add to the generalizations that they have been learning about patterns in the middle of words. **What did you learn from this sort to add to our generalizations? How can that help you as a reader and speller? How do you know where to split three consonants into syllables?** (The blend or digraph has to remain together: *ath-lete, pil-grim*.)

Extend: Complete standard weekly routines with these words. In a word hunt, it will be hard for students to find many more VV words that split between the vowels, but they may find words like *reason* that fit the VVCV pattern; encourage students to list them under that pattern for contrast. There are many VCCCV words that end in *-le* (*settle,* for example) that can be added in a word hunt. (The study of words that end in *-le* is explored more in later sorts.) For a weekly assessment, select at least 10 words for students to spell.

Apply: Select words from below to prepare a list for students to read. Have them watch for blends and digraphs to guide the syllable split in a word like *enchant* or *purchase*. Spelling these words is not as challenging as it may seem because careful listening reveals the sounds. The words *idea* and *area* are interesting because they have three syllables yet are very short words.

Additional Words: *actress, address, enchant, laughter, paddle, settle, sandwich, constant, complain, instant, merchant, ostrich, orchard, orphan, purchase, subtract, boa, bias, fuel, chaos, liar, neon, trio, idea, violin, area.*

SORT 16   Syllable Juncture in VCCCV and VV Patterns

VCC/CV	VC/CCV	V/V
athlete	**pilgrim**	**create**
control	complete	children
poet	duet	pumpkin
monster	riot	mushroom
halfway	kitchen	trial
poem	English	hundred
cruel	giant	lion
kingdom	inspect	diet

Sort 17   Open and Closed Syllables and Inflected Endings

This sort is designed to help students see the relationship between the rules they learned for inflected endings and the syllable juncture patterns they have been studying in this unit. It reviews the inflected rules covered in Sorts 2–5 but uses the terms *open* and *closed* to talk about why the consonant doubles after a short vowel in the base word. Two sets of headers are provided for the two sorts.

Generalization: Double the final consonant in a base word ending in a single consonant when adding -*ing* and -*ed* to keep the vowel short and the syllable closed. When the vowel is long in the first syllable, it will be open when -*ed* and -*ing* are added and no doubling is needed.

VCV	VCCV	VVCV
hoping	**hopping**	**leaking**
quoted	plotting	greeted
racing	dusted	shouting
skated	skipped	floated
joking	pasted	needed
	panting	
	winning	
	hunted	
	telling	
	chatted	
	wrapping	

Sorting and Discussion:

1. Cut off or cover the headers and quickly read through the words in this sort, talking about any that might be unfamiliar. Then ask, **What do you notice about these words? What has happened to the base word in some cases? Why?** Encourage responses that include the sounds of the vowels and patterns in the middle of the words as well as the endings and rules for adding the ending to base words.
2. Ask, **How can we sort these words?** Take different suggestions, but sort first by the juncture patterns (VCV, VCCV, and VVCV) because that is what students have been doing in this unit. **Let's start by sorting by the patterns in the middle.** Model how to sort a word in each category, and then sort the rest with student help.
3. Read down each column, emphasizing the first syllable. Ask, **How are the words in each**

column alike? Which words start with an open syllable? A closed syllable? Pull out *hoping* and *hopping* and ask, **Where would we break these words into syllables? What did you learn about adding** -*ing* **and** -*ed* **to words?**

4. Say, **Let's sort these words again under the double,** *e*-drop, **and nothing headers to review the rules for adding** -*ing* **and** -*ed*. **Remember to think about what has happened to the base word.** After sorting, read down each column and talk about the vowel sound and pattern in the middle. **If we did not double the** *p* **in** *hopping*, **how would we be likely to read that word?** (*hoping*) **Why?** (The first syllable would look open because it would not clearly end with a consonant.) **Why don't we double the last letter in a word like** *hunted*? (The first syllable is already closed because the base word is *hunt* and it already ends with two consonants.)

double	e-drop	nothing
hopping	hoping	dusted
plotting	quoted	panting
chatted	pasted	greeted
winning	racing	shouting
skipped	skated	floated
wrapping	joking	hunted
		leaking
		needed
		telling

Extend: Complete weekly routines. Have students record both sorts in their word study notebooks and write a statement about what they learned. Students should be able to find lots of words in a word hunt. Ask them to record them under the pattern headers to reinforce the link between juncture patterns and spelling rules for inflected endings. Call aloud some words from the sort but also words from the list below for students to apply what they have learned.

Apply: Give students base words from the list below like *doze, test, skim,* and so on, and ask them to add both -*ed* and -*ing* to them, applying the rules for adding inflected endings.

Additional Words: *doze, hire, note, pose, rate, fade, draft, link, shift, test, skim, scan, skip, clean, braid, cheat, heat, need.*

SORT 17   Open and Closed Syllables and Inflected Endings

VCV	VCCV	VVCV
e-drop	double	nothing
hoping	hopping	leaking
skipped	plotting	quoted
joking	wrapping	greeted
telling	winning	hunted
racing	chatted	shouting
skated	panting	floated
dusted	pasted	needed

UNIT REVIEW AND ASSESSMENT

Review:

Prepare a grand sort by making a copy of Sorts 13–17 for small groups of students. Have them work together to sort all the words under the syllable juncture pattern headers (VVCV, V/CV, VC/V, VCCV, VCCCV, and VV). Remind them to look for oddballs that do not fit the categories.

Review the generalizations that students have written for these sorts. The generalizations boil down to: Double consonants close the first syllable, making the vowel short (*but-ton, bas-ket, hop-ping, ath-lete*).

A single consonant can go with the first syllable to close the vowel (*vis-it, cab-in*) and keep it short, or with the second syllable, leaving the vowel open and long (*la-zy, ho-ping*). Double vowels stay together in most words like *rea-son* but can be split in some words like *ri-ot*. Readers need to be ready to try both.

Write pairs such as *super/supper, setting/seating, diner/dinner, Tigger/tiger, silly/silent*. Ask students to read the words, identify the patterns in the middle, and justify their pronunciation.

Assess:

Use the unit spell check on page 46 as a posttest to assess mastery.

Unit IV   Long-Vowel Patterns in Accented Syllables

NOTES FOR THE TEACHER

Background and Objectives

The vowel patterns studied in the within word pattern stage reappear in two-syllable words in these sorts. For example, the *ai* pattern in *rain* is also in *painter* and *complain*. Students will be introduced to the notion of accent or stress (we use these terms interchangeably) and helped to see that the long-vowel sound is clearly heard in the accented syllable. Sometimes students can "feel" the stress if they gently place the top of their hand or their thumb under their chin as they say the words.

Students may struggle to identify accent, and it may vary with regional dialects and language backgrounds. Do not be overly concerned about this, and allow students to put contested words into the oddball category. Being able to identify the stressed syllable is not the primary goal in these sorts. Stress is simply one more way to understand the regularity of the spelling system and how vowel sounds and vowel patterns are fairly reliable in stressed syllables. By attending to accent, students examine words from another perspective, which provides additional opportunities to learn and remember the spellings of specific words.

If you wish to address stress or accent directly, use students' names to introduce the concept. If their first name is Jennifer (JENnifer), for example, pronounce it with stress on the second syllable— JenNIFer—and ask why that sounds strange. As two-syllable homographs are encountered, discuss how you can tell them apart: PRESent (a gift) versus presENT (to introduce or give).

Some understanding of syllable stress will help students try alternative pronunciations when attempting to sound out an unfamiliar word or understand how to use the pronunciation guide for words they look up in the dictionary. It will also support students leaning English. Students will:

- Identify long-vowel patterns in accented syllables
- Spell the words in these sorts

Targeted Learners

These sorts are for students in the middle syllables and affixes stage of spelling who can spell single-syllable vowel patterns correctly for the most part but make mistakes in two-syllable words. They might spell *sailor* as SALOR or *favor* as FAIVOR. Many students will benefit from this review of vowel patterns, and students who have not learned to identify vowel patterns in earlier grades can learn how to do so now, in the context of these more difficult words. Neither the Elementary Spelling Inventory nor the Upper Level Spelling Inventory have many words with long vowels in accented syllables. This makes it especially important to use the unit spell check as a pretest to determine more accurately which students need to work on these words. Students who score 90% or better can move on to other features, but you may want to do Sort 23 to introduce the idea of accent or stress.

Teaching Tips

See the standard weekly routines listed on pages 6–8 to engage your students in repeated practice and extensions. Throughout this unit, students will be thinking about where accent falls as well as how words are broken into syllables. They can be asked to indicate syllable division and syllable stress in their word study notebooks by separating the syllables and underlining the accented syllables: <u>brace</u> let, a <u>wake</u>. Be sure to show students how stress is indicated in the dictionary. Some dictionaries use capital letters, bolded letters, or accent marks. For example, *parade* may appear as pa RADE, pə-rād', or pə-**rād**. Once words are sorted by the syllable that contains the vowel pattern, it is much easier to identify stressed syllables.

Learning about syllable division and accent are useful tools when reading and spelling unfamiliar words, but do not be overly concerned about accurately dividing all words into syllables—especially words students can already pronounce accurately. A word like *painter*, for example, could be divided as *paint-er* (base word plus suffix) or *pain-ter* (by sound), and either would be useful in pronouncing or spelling the word.

Keep dictionaries handy and encourage their use when questions arise. Most of the words in these sorts are familiar, but we suggest that you ask one or two students to look up the meanings of a few words to add to the introductory lesson. Some suggestions are given in the sorts that follow about the use of the dictionary and words that need some discussion.

You may want to talk about *syllable types* as you discuss the words in these sorts. In this unit, three of the six syllable types are covered as long-vowel patterns in the accented syllables: (1) open—the syllable is "open" because it ends with a long vowel (i.e., **pa**per, **rai**sin, or **pay**ment); (2) vowel-consonant-*e* (i.e, **bra**celet or mis**take**); and (3) vowel teams (**pain**ter or ex**plain**). Students will see some familiar base words in many of these words (e.g., de*light*, *light*ning). Point these out and talk about how longer words will be easier to spell when the base word is identified. Sometimes you may ask students to identify verbs and add -*ing*, -*ed*, or -*s* to review the rules introduced in earlier sorts. You may also ask students to identify nouns and write the plural forms. These can be written in their word study notebooks. At other times, you may review compound words or syllable juncture patterns.

When students go on word hunts for vowel sounds, welcome single-syllable words as well as two-syllable words because they will confirm that the same patterns are used to spell the sounds. Finding additional words with these same patterns may be challenging in some cases, so do not hold students accountable for finding any certain number of them in a word hunt. Instead, you may want to focus on creating class lists that are added to throughout the unit.

Because there is often no way to know what long pattern to use when spelling an unfamiliar word (Is it *exclame* or *exclaim*?), we can't recommend asking students to spell unstudied words in the weekly assessment. However, see the "Apply" section in each lesson for ideas.

Games from Chapter 6 of *Words Their Way* that feature vowel patterns should work here. *Stressbusters*, a game described in Chapter 7 of *Words Their Way*, can be used throughout this unit with different words each week.

Examining syllable breaks and accent can support pronunciation for English learners as you model how to emphasize syllables that they may not be used to stressing. English tends to accent initial syllables more than final syllables, but this is not true in other languages, such as Spanish. Reading down the columns of words and pairing up English learners with native English speakers will reinforce pronunciation.

UNIT SPELL CHECK 4 ASSESSMENT FOR LONG-VOWEL PATTERNS IN ACCENTED SYLLABLES

Call the words below for students to spell on a sheet of notebook paper. Use in sentences as needed to clarify meaning.

1. complain	**2.** soapy	**3.** season
4. Tuesday	**5.** fifteen	**6.** owner
7. highway	**8.** awake	**9.** explode
10. freedom	**11.** refuse	**12.** balloon
13. invite	**14.** sweater	**15.** poster
16. payment	**17.** advice	**18.** compete
19. eastern	**20.** scooter	

Interpreting Scores on Pre- and Posttests

Use the goal-setting form on page 4 to analyze and record results, and use the pacing guide on page 5 to plan which sorts to use.

- **90% or better**—Students can move on to the next unit, but consider doing Sort 23, which covers most of the patterns and reviews or introduces the idea of vowel sounds in stressed syllables.
- **75% to 85%**—A "gray area" where teacher judgment is needed. Examine the types of errors students make to see if there are particular vowels that can be targeted rather than doing all the sorts.
- **70% or less**—Students will benefit from doing all the sorts in the unit.

Sort 18   Long *A* Patterns in Accented Syllables

Students will be asked to look at words in a new way in this sort, so we recommend using a teacher-directed sort with lots of opportunity to talk about the features of the words. The second sort by patterns might be done on a second day.

Generalization: In a two-syllable word, one syllable is stressed or accented. The long *a* sound in two-syllable words is spelled with open *a*, *ai*, *ay*, and *a-e* patterns.

1st	2nd	oddball
baby	**awake**	
painter	parade	again*
raisin	complain	
crayon	decay	
flavor	mistake	
maybe	obey	
bracelet	escape	
grateful	amaze	
basic	today*	
fable	explain	
waiter	remain	
payment		

*High-frequency word

Sorting and Discussion:

1. Read over the words quickly and discuss any that might be unfamiliar, such as *decay*. Ask, **What do you notice about this collection of words?** Probe with, **What vowel sound do you hear in all the words?** Students should notice that most words have the long sound of *a*. **Which syllable has the long *a* sound?** (Sometimes the first and sometimes the last.)

2. Explain, **We will sort these words in a new way. Listen to each syllable and decide where you hear the long *a* sound.** Put up the two headers and introduce the key words: *Baby* **has the long *a* sound in the first syllable.** *Awake* **has long *a* in the second syllable.** Sort the rest of the words with the students' help. Alert them to watch for oddballs.

3. After sorting, explain, **As we read down this column, listen how we put a little more emphasis on the first syllable. We call this the stressed or accented syllable. Read these with me.**

Repeat with the second column. Sometimes students can "feel" the stress if they gently place the top of their hand under their chin as they say the words. Talk about the oddballs. **Why did we put *again* under oddballs?** (It does not have the long *a* sound.)

4. Ask, **Do you see another way to sort these words?** Probe if necessary with, **What vowel patterns do you see in the words?** Compliment students if they point out syllable patterns, but explain, **Let's sort by the long *a* pattern, which may be in the first or second syllable.** Set up *baby*, *daily*, *awake*, and *crayon* as key words. Sort the rest of the words with the students' help. *Obey* will be an additional oddball because it has the sound of long *a* but not one of the patterns.

baby	daily	awake	crayon	oddball
flavor	raisin	bracelet	payment	
basic	waiter	escape	maybe	again*
fable	explain	mistake	decay	obey
	complain	parade	today	
	remain	amaze		
		grateful		

5. Read down each column to listen for the vowel sound and check the pattern. **What is the pattern in each column?** Underline the patterns in the key words as shown above. Ask, **Which syllable is accented or stressed?** (The one with the long *a* pattern.)

6. Help students draw some conclusions by asking, **What did you learn from this sort?** Talk about how familiar patterns show up in two-syllable words and how the long-vowel sound can be heard in the accented syllable.

Extend: Students should work with the words using the standard weekly routines on pages 6–8. During a word hunt, they may find words with the long *a* pattern and sound that are not stressed, such as *locate*, *essay*, or *dictate*. These words can still be added to the pattern sorts. Call at least 10 words for an end-of-week assessment.

Ask students to look up some of the words in a dictionary to see how accent or stress is indicated in the pronunciation guide. As we have noted, dictionaries differ. Students can then be asked to break their words into syllables and indicate the accented syllables with an accent mark or by underlining. This can become a new routine to do throughout this unit in their word study notebooks.

Ask students to identify the syllable juncture patterns in some words. Open syllables include: *dai-ly, pay-ment* (VVCV), *ba-by, fla-vor* (VCV), and closed syllables include: *mis-take* (VCCV). Ask students to review rules from Unit II by adding *-ing* and *-ed* to words such as *amaze* (*amazed, amazing*), *decay* (*decayed, decaying*), *obey* (*obeyed, obeying*), *escape* (*escaped, escaping*), and *explain* (*explained, explaining*).

Apply: Select some words from the given list that are less familiar and ask students to read them. Ask, **What can help you read these words?** (Look for familiar vowel patterns in the first or second syllable.) Ask students to spell some words that you call aloud from the list (e.g., *trainer, basement, vibrate, delay*) and ask, **What can help you spell these words?** Thinking of a base word can help sometimes, as can remembering that words ending in the long *a* sound are usually spelled with *-ay*. However, there is no way to be sure of the pattern in *vibrate*— it could be *ai* or *a-e*.

Additional Words: *lazy, bacon, wafer, favor, crater, daisy, dainty, trainer, rainbow, straighten, sprained, railroad, vibrate, grateful, pavement, baseball, basement, crusade, insane, embrace, prayer, hooray, betray, mayor, player, dismay, delay, sustain, exclaim, contain, refrain, terrain, regain*; oddballs: *captain, bargain, garbage*.

SORT 18   Long *A* Patterns in Accented Syllables

1st	**2nd**	*oddball*
baby	**awake**	painter
waiter	obey	raisin
complain	decay	crayon
mistake	fable	parade
flavor	maybe	basic
escape	bracelet	amaze
again	today	grateful
explain	payment	remain

Sort 19   Long *i* Patterns in Accented Syllables

Generalization: In a two-syllable word, one syllable is stressed or accented. The long *i* sound in two-syllable words is spelled with open *i*, *igh*, and *i-e* patterns.

1st	2nd	oddball
frighten	**divide**	machine
lightning	delight	city
rival	surprise	
crisis	decide	
slightly	advice	
minus	combine	
highway	survive	
brightly	invite	
Friday	tonight	
idol	describe	
ninety	polite	

Explore Meaning: Display the word *rival* (competitor) and ask, **How would you break this word into syllables? Is it *riv-al* or *ri-val*? Why?** Talk about the meaning and offer examples like a "rival soccer team." You might show the pronunciation guide in a dictionary and talk about where it is split into syllables and where the accent falls: rī′ vəl or rī vəl.

Sorting and Discussion:

1. Read over the words quickly and discuss *rival* as described above. If students have trouble pronouncing any of the words, set them aside for later or talk about likely places to split words into syllables. Then ask, **What do you notice about all of these words? Which syllable is accented or stressed in *rival*?** (The first.) **What is the sound of *i* in the first syllable?** (Long *i*.) Repeat this with the word *divide*.

2. Explain, **Last week we sorted long *a* words by the stressed syllable, and this week we will sort long *i* words. Listen to each syllable and decide where you hear the long *i* sound.** Put up the two headers and introduce the key words: **Frighten has the long *i* sound in the first syllable. Divide has long *i* in the second syllable.** Sort the rest of the words with the students' help and alert them to listen for oddballs.

3. After sorting, read down each column, emphasizing the accented syllable. Ask, **What do you notice about the words in each column?** Review the term *accent* or *stress* and talk about how to detect it, but do not be too concerned if students do not master this. The accented syllable is also the syllable where the long *i* sound is heard. **What are the oddballs and why?** (They do not have the long *i* sound.) Ask, **Why is Friday capitalized?**

4. **Do you see another way to sort these words? What can we use as key words? Why?** Underline key words or the pattern in the words and sort together, or ask students to sort their own words independently. After sorting, read down each column to check and review the pattern. **How are these words all alike? What can we say about the oddballs now?** Talk about the syllable pattern in *city* (VCV) and where the syllable break would be for each one (*cit-y*). Compare them to *mi-nus* and *Fri-day*. Review with students how they learned that the VCV pattern can be either open or closed depending on whether the vowel sound is long or short.

5. Ask, **What did you learn from this sort?** Help students state a generalization about how the stressed syllable has the long *i* sound, which is spelled three different ways in these words. Add this to the generalization from the last sort.

Sort by Long *i* Patterns

minus	frighten	divide	oddball
idol	slightly	surprise	machine
Friday	lightning	decide	city
rival	highway	advice	
crisis	brightly	survive	
	delight	combine	
	tonight	invite	
		describe	
		polite	
		ninety	

Extend: Students should work with the words using the standard weekly routines on pages 6–8. Not all the words in the sort will fit the syllable patterns studied in the last unit, but you can review by asking students to mark the syllable breaks and patterns in these words: *ri-val, si-lent, Fri-day* (V/CV), *fin-ish, cit-y* (VC/V), *ad-vice* (VCCV), *sur-prise*, and *des-cribe* (VCCCV). Assess by calling at least 10 words aloud as in a traditional spelling test.

Apply: Ask students to find words that contain a base word (e.g., *frighten, brightly, tonight*). Ask, **What would help you spell *tightly* or *lighter*?** Ask, **How can you tell which pattern to use when there is no base word?** Suggest that they spell a word several ways to see which one might look "right" or "familiar." Generating spellings is necessary to help them locate the correct spelling in a dictionary.

Additional Words: *diner, writer, tiger, pirate, private, pilot, spider, visor, lively, nightmare, tighten, excite, confide, recline, collide, despite, beside, driveway, arrive, provide, advise, ignite, despite, divine, resign, design.*

SORT 19   Long *I* Patterns in Accented Syllables

1st	**2**nd	*oddball*
frighten	**divide**	surprise
decide	advice	machine
survive	crisis	combine
minus	city	slightly
ninety	invite	Friday
describe	lightning	polite
rival	tonight	brightly
delight	idol	highway

Sort 20 Long *O* Patterns in Accented Syllables

By now, students should be able to sort the words independently by syllables and patterns.

Generalization: The accented syllable with the long *o* sound is spelled with *open o, oa, ow,* and *o-e* patterns.

1st	2nd	oddball
toaster	below	Europe
pony	explode	
lonely	suppose	
owner	compose	
lower	decode	
lonesome	remote	
loafer	alone	
frozen	approach	
soapy	awoke	
bowling	erode	
sofa		
robot		
coaster		

Explore Meaning: Write the word *remote* and talk about where to make a syllable break to read it (Is it *re-mote* or *rem-ote*?) and what it means to the students. How is it related to *remote control*? Ask a student to look it up in the dictionary and talk about the definition. Repeat with *erode*. Talk about the two meanings of *loafer* (a kind of shoe or a kind of person who loafs around or takes it easy).

Sorting and Discussion:

1. Read over the words quickly and discuss words as described above. If students have trouble pronouncing any of the words, talk about how to split words into syllables. Ask, **What do you notice about these words? How can we sort them?** Students should be able to sort independently by the accented syllables and where they hear the long *o* sound. Remind them, **Watch out for an oddball.**
2. After sorting, tell students, **Read down each column to check for the sound and accent. What can you say about the words in each column? What is the oddball?** (*Europe*) **Why is it odd?** (The long *o* pattern is in the unaccented syllable and is not pronounced as a long *o*.) **Why do we capitalize it?** (Because it is a proper noun.) Ask, **Can you find three words that have the same base word?** (*lonely, lonesome,* and *alone*) Talk about how they are related in meaning.

3. Ask, **How else can you sort these words?** Let students find their own headers and sort independently. After sorting, ask, **What are the patterns for long o?** Have students indicate the patterns or underline the words to create key words to use each time for sorting. **What did you learn from this sort?** Help students state a generalization about how the stressed syllable has the long *o* sound, which is spelled four different ways in these words. Add this to the list of generalizations for this unit.

pony	toaster	below	explode	oddball
frozen	loafer	owner	lonely	Europe
sofa	soapy	lower	lonesome	
robot	approach	bowling	erode	
	coaster		suppose	
			compose	
			decode	
			remote	
			alone	
			awoke	

Extend: Students should work with the words using the standard weekly routines on pages 6–8. Ask students to write their own generalization for this sort in their word study notebooks. They should be able to do this after writing a group generalization in earlier sorts. Assess by calling at least 10 words for students to spell. Because there is no way to know what long *o* pattern to use when spelling an unfamiliar word (Is it *tadpoal* or *tadpole*? *Doenate* or *donate*?), we can't recommend asking students to spell unstudied words in the weekly assessment.

Select some words from the sort with the VCCV pattern for students to divide into syllables: *sup-pose, com-pose.* Repeat with VCV words such as *fro-zen, so-fa,* and *ro-bot.*

Apply: Remind students about how breaking the word into syllables helps them read unfamiliar words and then show them some additional words to divide and read, such as *bony, donate, tadpole, oppose,* and *oatmeal.*

Additional Words: *bony, chosen, donate, notice, soda, total, potion, rotate, stolen, cocoa, hopeful, notebook, rowboat, mower, coastal, oatmeal, enclose, disown, tadpole, expose, oppose, console.* The VCC vowel pattern is found in *soldier, poster, postage, molding, hostess, enroll, behold,* and *revolt.*

SORT 20   Long *O* Patterns in Accented Syllables

1st	2nd	*oddball*
toaster	**below**	coaster
alone	pony	explode
sofa	suppose	lonely
compose	owner	decode
lower	remote	lonesome
approach	loafer	awoke
frozen	soapy	Europe
bowling	erode	robot

Sort 21   Long *U* Patterns in Accented Syllables

Generalization: The accented syllable with the long *u* sound is spelled with open *u, ew, oo,* and *o-e* patterns.

1st	2nd
rooster	**include**
Tuesday	cocoon
useful	amuse
jewel	confuse
doodle	reduce
toothache	balloon
noodle	cartoon
scooter	raccoon
beauty	shampoo
chewy	
fewer	
tulip	
music	
ruler	
student	

Explore Meaning: *Ruler* has two meanings to discuss (a person in charge, like a king, or something to measure with). Assign a student to look up the word in advance of the discussion.

Sorting and Discussion:

1. Students should be able to do this sort independently by accented syllables if they have already done previous sorts. Bring them together to talk about word meaning as needed and check in about reading the words. Ask, **Was there any word you were not sure how to read? What did you do to help figure it out?** Let someone demonstrate how to split such words into syllables.
2. After sorting, remind students, **Read down each column to check for the sound and accent. What can you say about the words in each column?**

3. Have students sort a second time by the vowel patterns in the words, and warn them to look out for some oddballs. Ask, **What patterns did you find for long *u*? What are the oddballs? Why do we capitalize Tuesday?** Ask, **Can you find a compound word?** (*toothache; useful* might also be mentioned, as in "full of use," but it is not a true compound because the spelling of *full* is not complete. Instead, the *-ful* is a suffix.)

ruler	jewel	rooster	include	oddball
music	fewer	cocoon	useful	Tuesday
tulip	chewy	doodle	amuse	beauty
student		toothache	confuse	
		noodle	reduce	
		scooter		
		balloon		
		cartoon		
		raccoon		
		shampoo		

Extend: Students should work with the words using the standard weekly routines on pages 6–8. Assess by calling at least 10 words for students to spell.

Apply: Ask students how to spell a word they might not know like *baboon*. Record all possible answers, and talk about the reasons for their choices. Does the *b* double as in *babbune*? Is the final syllable *-bune* or *-bewn* or *-boon*? They can ask themselves, "Does it look right?" But explain that sometimes, when there are different possibilities, they might need to check a dictionary. Ask a volunteer to look up the correct spelling.

Additional Words: *ruby, super, tuna, future, humid, unit, rumor, tutor, fluid, dual, duet, fluent, sewer, steward, pewter, moody, spoonful, foolish, poodle, lagoon, baboon, tattoo, maroon, conclude, perfume, consume, compute, exclude, salute, dispute, abuse, excuse.*

SORT 21   Long *U* Patterns in Accented Syllables

1st	**2nd**	*oddball*
rooster	**include**	Tuesday
reduce	balloon	useful
cartoon	doodle	fewer
jewel	ruler	raccoon
toothache	music	noodle
beauty	shampoo	student
chewy	scooter	confuse
cocoon	tulip	amuse

Sort 22   Long *E* Patterns in Accented Syllables

This sort is a little different because it includes the short sound of *e* (spelled *ea* as in *feather*) as well as the long sound.

Generalization: The accented syllable with the long *e* sound is spelled with open *e*, *ea*, *ee*, and *e-e* patterns; *ea* can also represent the short sound of *e*.

Sort by Accented Syllable

1st long	1st short	2nd long
needle	**feather**	**succeed**
even	steady	fifteen
fever	healthy	thirteen
season	leather	supreme
freedom	heavy	repeat
meter	pleasant	compete
eastern	sweater	defeat
people		extreme
meaning		

Explore Meaning: *Season* has two distinct meanings ("time of year" or "to flavor").

Sorting and Discussion:

1. Read over the words quickly and talk about the meanings as needed. Expect some confusion about how to read words with the *ea* pattern, but encourage students to try both long and short *e* as they would with words like *read*. Ask, **What do you notice about the words for this week?** Take many ideas, but be sure to talk about how the words have both long and short *e* sounds, which is different from the sorts students have been doing earlier in this unit.
2. Explain, **We will sort by the accented syllable, but we also have to listen to the sound of *e*.** Set up the three headers and sort the words with the students' help. After sorting, check by reading down each column, emphasizing the stressed syllable. Ask, **What do you notice about the words in each column?** Help students see that the same principles apply: In the stressed syllable, we can clearly hear the vowel sound, whether it is long or short.

3. Ask, **How can we sort these in a different way?** Students should be able to do a pattern sort independently, but bring them together to talk about the patterns they found. Ask, **What can we conclude about this sort?** Help them state a generalization.

<u>e</u>ven	n<u>ee</u>dle	comp<u>e</u>te
fever	succeed	extreme
meter	fifteen	supreme
	thirteen	
	freedom	
season	**f<u>ea</u>ther**	**oddball**
defeat	leather	people*
repeat	heavy	
meaning	pleasant	
eastern	sweater	
	steady	
	healthy	

Extend: Students should work with the words using the standard weekly routines on pages 6–8. Display numerical terms from *thirteen* to *nineteen* and ask, **Is there anything you notice about the spelling of these words?** (*Thirteen* and *fifteen* differ from the others, which simply add *-teen* to a number word (*four-teen*, *six-teen*, *seven-teen*, and *nine-teen*). *Eighteen* adds only *-een*, but the spelling of the first syllable remains the same.

Apply: Select words from below such as *legal*, *metal*, *reason*, and *steady*. Display them first as just the words, and talk about how it can be hard to know whether the *e* is long or short. Then display them in simple sentences to help students see how context and a flexible decoding strategy can help them identify the word: It is not *legal* to steal. Gold is a *metal*. Give me a good *reason*. Hold the chair *steady*.

Additional Words: *zebra, legal, veto, prefix, tepee, evil, freezer, indeed, breezy, cheetah, steeple, tweezers, beetle, feeble, greedy, sweeten, reader, easel, reason, feature, creature, treaty, eagle, eager, cleaner, increase, canteen, agree, degree, between, complete, trapeze, athlete, stampede, conceal, ideal, ready, steady, weather, sweaty, jealous, weapon, heaven, meadow, breakfast, instead;* CVC with short *e*: *metal, level, lemon, seven.*

SORT 22   Long *E* Patterns in Accented Syllables

1st long	1st short	2nd long
needle	**feather**	**succeed**
season	even	leather
compete	repeat	defeat
fever	heavy	freedom
pleasant	meaning	meter
extreme	fifteen	sweater
eastern	steady	healthy
people	supreme	thirteen

Sort 23   Review of Long-Vowel Patterns in Accented Syllables

This is an optional sort that you might use after doing the other sorts in this unit, or you might use it for students who scored in the 85% to 90% range on the pretest and need only an introduction to the idea of stress before tackling the next unit.

Generalization: The long-vowel sound is clearly heard in the accented syllable of a two-syllable word and is usually spelled with familiar vowel patterns seen in one-syllable words.

Sort by Accented Syllable

1st	2nd	oddball
lazy	**contain**	
moody	debate	
lighter	stampede	
speaker	delay	
ruby	invade	
closely	salute	
visor	expose	
foolish	provide	
safety		
bony		
soda		
waitress		
slowly		
freezer		
zebra		
eagle		

Explore Meaning: *Speaker* indicates a person who is talking as well as a mechanical device for transmitting sound. *Soda* has multiple meanings. Talk about generic terms for carbonated drinks or soft drinks, and explain that this term varies in different parts of the country (*soda* in the Northeast, *pop* in the northern Midwest, *coke* in the South).

Sorting and Discussion:

1. If students have not done previous sorts in this unit, we recommend doing this as a teacher-directed sort in which you introduce the idea of accented syllables. Read over the words quickly, talking about any that might be unfamiliar.

If students find it difficult reading a word, take suggestions about how to break it into syllables. If this is a review unit, you might let students sort independently by stress and then bring them together to discuss and guide the pattern sort in step 4.

2. Ask, **What do you notice about these words?** Take a variety of responses, but then explain, **We are going to sort these two-syllable words by where we hear the long-vowel sound.** Introduce the headers and key words, and sort the rest of the words with student help.

3. After sorting, explain, **As we read down this column, listen how we put a little more emphasis on the first syllable. We call this the stressed or accented syllable. Read these with me.** Repeat with the second column. Sometimes students can "feel" the stress if they gently place the top of their hand under their chin as they say the words. **What is the oddball and why?**

4. Explain, **When the syllable is accented, we can clearly hear the long-vowel sound.** Ask, **What do you notice about the spelling of the long-vowel sounds? Do you see some familiar patterns? We are going to sort next by pattern, but there are a lot of different patterns. Could we put *speaker* and *waitress* in the same category? Why?** (They both have a vowel pair or VV pattern.) **Do you see some others we could put together?** Take student suggestions, or pick a pair and ask students to tell you how they are alike.

5. **Let's pick some key words and label them.** (See suggestions below.) **Remember to look for the pattern in the accented syllable.** Sort the rest of the words with student help. First identify the accented syllable and then the pattern. Some words may not have any category, and they can go in oddballs for now.

Sort by Syllable Pattern

lazy open V	speaker VV	debate VCe	oddball
soda	moody	closely	lighter
visor	waitress	safety	slowly
ruby	foolish	invade	delay
zebra	freezer	stampede	
bony	contain	salute	
	eagle	provide	
		expose	

6. Ask, **What do you notice about each column? Look at the oddballs. Which ones have familiar patterns?** Explain, **The spellings are not really odd, but they have no category in this sort. Which one is really odd and why?** Help students draw some conclusions by asking, **What did you learn from this sort?** Talk about how familiar patterns show up in two-syllable words and how the long-vowel sound can be heard in the accented syllable.

Extend: Students can complete standard routines. A word hunt should focus on finding long-vowel patterns in accented syllables. Ask students to write their own generalization in their word study notebooks, and provide help as needed. Ask students to divide their words into syllables. Which ones fit the syllable patterns covered in Unit III, and which ones are new? (*Slow-ly* and *close-ly* are new with the VV or VCe pattern in the first syllable.

Debate and *delay* do not have a long vowel in the first syllable.)

Apply: Ask students how to spell a word they might not know like *canteen*, *relief*, or *explain*. Record all answers and talk about the reasons for their choices. They might ask themselves "Does it look right?" But explain that sometimes, when there are several possibilities, they just need to check a dictionary. Ask volunteers to look up the correct spellings.

Additional Words: See previous lists of additional words in this unit.

UNIT ASSESSMENT

Use the unit spell check as a posttest to assess mastery of these features and words.

SORT 23   Review of Long-Vowel Patterns in Accented Syllables

1st	2nd	*oddball*
lazy	**contain**	soda
moody	closely	waitress
debate	visor	slowly
lighter	foolish	freezer
speaker	safety	zebra
ruby	invade	eagle
stampede	bony	expose
delay	salute	provide

Unit V   Other Vowel Patterns in Accented Syllables

NOTES FOR THE TEACHER

Background and Objectives

In these sorts, students will revisit "other" vowel patterns (*r*-influenced vowels, ambiguous vowels, and diphthongs) in two-syllable words. They will continue to learn about the notion of accent or stress (we use these terms interchangeably) and how the vowel sound is clearly heard in the accented syllable.

Some understanding of syllable stress will help students try alternative pronunciations when attempting to sound out an unfamiliar word or understand how to use the pronunciation guide for words they look up in the dictionary. In the next unit, they will learn about the unaccented syllable, so understanding the accented syllable will make this more comprehensible. Students will:

- Identify other vowel patterns in accented syllables, including *r*-influenced vowels and diphthongs
- Spell the words in these sorts

Targeted Learners

These sorts are for students in the middle syllables and affixes stage of spelling, who will benefit from a review of other vowels at the same time they learn about accent and two-syllable words. They might spell *serving* as SURVING or *shower* as SHOUER. Use the unit spell check to determine more accurately which students need to work on these words. Students who score 90% or better can move on to other features.

Teaching Tips

See the standard weekly routines listed on pages 6–8 to engage your students in repeated practice and extensions. Throughout this unit, students will be thinking about where accent falls as well as how words are broken into syllables. Sometimes students can "feel" the stress if they gently place the back of their hand or their thumb under their chin as they say the words, but do not be overly concerned if they do not master detecting stress. It is simply one more way to understand the regularity of the spelling system and how vowel sounds and vowel patterns are fairly reliable in stressed syllables. If you wish to address stress directly, use students' names and two-syllable homographs (see *Words Their Way: Word Study for Phonics, Vocabulary, and Spelling Instruction*).

You may want to refer to *syllable types* as you guide students' examination of the words in these sorts. In this unit, two of the six syllable types are covered as vowel patterns in accented syllables: vowel teams (including diphthongs and ambiguous vowels in words such as *avoid*, *destroy*, and *country*) and *r*-controlled vowels (*partner, repair*).

Students can be asked to indicate syllable division and syllable stress in their word study notebook by underlining the accented syllables: *noi sy*, *a mount*. Be sure to show students how stress is indicated in the dictionary. Some dictionaries use bolded letters and others use accent marks: noi' zē, **noi** zē. Dictionaries show syllable division in both the bolded entry word and the pronunciation guide, and they may differ (i.e., **car ry** [kar' ē]), so this is not an exact process. Learning how to divide words into syllables is a useful tool when reading and spelling unfamiliar words, but students need not master it or be expected to decide on syllable divisions for all words in a sort.

Learning rules about where to hyphenate words at the end of a line is not nearly as important as it once was, but look for examples of such words in students' reading materials. Point out how the hyphen comes at a syllable break and not at just any place in the word. Talk about how students might sometimes need to do this in their own writing and demonstrate how it is done.

Remember that students may not always agree about the exact sound in a word because of variations in dialect and language backgrounds. This is especially true of the diphthongs (*out*, *toy*) and consonant-influenced vowels (*watch*, *warm*) in these sorts. Be ready to accept these differences and listen carefully to alternative pronunciations so you can help students sort by their own dialect. You may also find regional differences in word usage and vocabulary. Does water come from a *tap*, *faucet*, or *spigot* in your area? Are big sandwiches *subs*, *heroes*, or *grinders*? *Crayon* is pronounced as a one-syllable word in some regions, and we don't agree about the first vowel in *pecan*. Discuss and celebrate these differences. You can talk about "conventional" or dictionary pronunciations without labeling a pronunciation as right or wrong.

Keep dictionaries handy and encourage their use when questions arise. Some of the words in these sorts will not be well known, and students should be encouraged to look up the meanings of words to add to the introductory discussion for each sort. Some suggestions are given in the sorts that follow about particular words and the use of the dictionary for specific features. Try to revisit any unfamiliar words during the week and look for opportunities to use them. Multiple exposures are needed for students to master new vocabulary.

When students go on word hunts for vowel sounds, welcome single-syllable words as well as two-syllable words because they will confirm that the same patterns are used to spell the sounds. Finding additional words with these same patterns may sometimes be challenging for students, so do not hold them accountable for finding any certain number of them in a word hunt. Instead, you may want to focus on creating group lists that students add to throughout the unit.

Games from Chapter 6 of *Words Their Way* that feature vowel patterns should work here. *Stressbusters*, a game described in Chapter 7, can be used throughout this unit with different words each week. *Stressed Out*, a game described in Unit IV, works well with these features.

For English learners, there may be a number of unfamiliar words in a sort and words that may be difficult to pronounce. The meaning of a few words can be discussed each day rather than presenting them all at once. Students can sometimes identify cognates to learn about the words they do not know. For example, Spanish speakers might recognize that the words *adhere* and *adherirse* are cognates. Help students to generate related words and phrases to study the meaning of words. The websites Onelook and Visuwords can be helpful.

UNIT SPELL CHECK 5 ASSESSMENT FOR *R*-INFLUENCED AND AMBIGUOUS VOWELS IN ACCENTED SYLLABLES

For a pretest or posttest, call the words aloud for students to spell on a sheet of notebook paper. Use in sentences if necessary to clarify meaning.

1. noisy	2. autumn	3. barber
4. forest	5. quarter	6. person
7. nearby	8. thousand	9. before
10. awful	11. repair	12. amount
13. sincere	14. worry	15. thirty
16. early	17. Thursday	18. destroy
19. always	20. rarely	

Interpreting Scores on Pre- and Posttests

Use the goal-setting form on page 4 to analyze and record results, and use the pacing guide on page 5 to plan which sorts to use.

- **90% or better**—Students can move on to the next unit.
- **75% to 85%**—A "gray area" where teacher judgment is needed. Examine the types of errors students make to see if there are particular vowel patterns that can be targeted rather than doing all the sorts.
- **70% or less**—Students will benefit from doing all the sorts in the unit.

Sort 24   *OY/OI* and *OU/OW* in Accented Syllables

Generalization: Familiar vowel patterns (*oy, oi, ow, ou*) show up in two-syllable words and can be clearly heard in the accented syllable. *Oy* and *ow* spelling patterns usually occur at the end of a syllable; *oi* and *ou* usually occur in syllables ending with a consonant.

Sort by Accented Syllable

accented 1st	accented 2nd
voyage	destroy
shower	appoint
loyal	avoid
poison	annoy
noisy	employ
drowsy	about*
trouble	amount
country	around*
double	
tower	
southern	
county	
counter	
thousand	
coward	
powder	

*High-frequency word

Explore Meaning: The word *counter* has several different meanings (a person or instrument that counts, the level surface on kitchen cabinets, but also opposed to or against). *Country* also has multiple meanings (a rural area or a nation). Talk about the difference between *county* (divisions in a state) and *country*.

Sorting and Discussion:

1. Read over the words quickly and discuss any that might be unfamiliar or that have multiple meanings. Ask, **What do you notice about this collection of words?** Probe with, **What vowel sounds do you hear? How could we sort these words?** Accept different possibilities. Remind students, **We have been sorting by the accented or stressed syllable, so let's start that way again.** Put up the two headers and model how to sort one word into each: *Voyage* is accented **on the first syllable, and** *about* **is accented on the second.** Sort the rest of the words with the students' help.

2. After sorting, check, **As we read down this column, listen to how we accent the first syllable. Read these with me.** Repeat with the second column. Sometimes students can "feel" the stress if they gently place the top of their hand under their chin as they say the words.

3. Ask, **How else can we sort these words?** Students should mention the different vowel patterns and sounds. Use bolded key words, and underline the patterns to use as headers. You can also mark the short *u* in the word *coŭntry*. **What do you notice about the** *ou* **pattern?** Compare the sound in *about* and *country*. Sort the words with student help.

4. After sorting, read down each column to check for sound and ask, **What do you notice about the words in this column? Where does the** *oy* **(and** *ow***) sound come?** (Only at the end of a syllable.) **Where does** *oi* **(and** *ou***) come?** (Only within a syllable.) **How can this help you read and spell words?** Talk about how familiar vowel patterns will help them read and spell two-syllable words. Be sure to use the "Apply" activity below to reinforce this. Have students mark their own set of headers and sort under your direction if time allows.

vo*yay*	n*oisy*	dr*ow*sy	ab*ou*t*	c*oŭ*ntry
annoy	poison	shower	county	trouble
employ	appoint	tower	counter	double
loyal	avoid	coward	amount	southern
destroy		powder	thousand	
			around	

Extend: Have students sort by both accented syllable and vowel patterns and sounds, but do not be concerned if the students make errors in the accent sort. This can be difficult for some students and is not something they need to master. Complete standard weekly routines described on pages 6–8. Send students on a word hunt to find more words that will fit into these categories. Welcome single-syllable words as well because they will confirm that the same patterns are showing up.

Focus on the unaccented initial *a*. **What do you notice about the first syllable in** *about*? (It sounds like /uh/.) **Can you find some more words that start with this same sound?** (*annoy, appoint, about, amount,* and *around*) Students might remember studying words like these in the late within word pattern sorts. **What syllable is accented in all these words? What makes these hard for the speller?** (The *a* is not long or short but sounds like /uh/. Some have a double consonant after the *a*.) **Note:** In the next unit, students will learn about the *schwa* sound /ə/, and Sort 41 focuses on these unaccented initial syllables in detail.

Apply: Talk about how looking for the vowel pattern and dividing the word into syllables can help students decode unfamiliar words. Compare words like *shadow* and *prowler* or *cousin* and *fountain*, and talk about how students may need to try two sounds.

Putting the words into sentences will show how context helps: *The prowler hid in the shadow. I got a drink from the water fountain.* Call some words aloud for students to spell such as *ahoy, joyful,* or *rejoice* and identify whether the /oi/ sound is in the middle or at the end of a syllable as a guide to choosing from *oy* or *oi*. Repeat with two words such as *rowdy* and *bounty*.

Additional Words: *joyful, royal, oyster, boycott, soybean, enjoy, ahoy, toilet, moisture, ointment, pointed, exploit, rejoice, turmoil, turquoise, prowler, brownie, rowdy, trowel, towel, council, lousy, scoundrel, bounty, voucher, trousers, profound, surround, announce, youngster, famous, nervous, mountain.*

SORT 24   *OY/OI* and *OU/OW* in Accented Syllables

1st	2nd	
voyage	**about**	**drowsy**
noisy	**country**	destroy
coward	amount	thousand
avoid	poison	trouble
tower	annoy	employ
shower	double	loyal
county	around	powder
appoint	counter	southern

Sort 25 AU, AW, and AL in Accented Syllables

These words are all accented on the first syllable, so there is no sort by stress. Students can sort these independently by vowel pattern, but bring the students together to talk about word meanings and generalizations.

Generalization: Familiar vowel patterns (*au*, *aw*, *al*) show up in two-syllable words and can be clearly heard in the accented syllable.

au	aw	al	oddball
saucer	**awful**	**also***	laughed
author	awkward	always*	allow
August	lawyer	walnut	
autumn	awesome	although	
laundry	flawless	alter	
caution	gawking	salty	
faucet			
sausage			
auction			
haunted			

Explore Meaning: This sort has a number of words that might be unfamiliar, but the concepts are probably familiar. Show a picture of a faucet and ask students what they call it. *Spigot* and *tap* are widely used in some areas of the country. Assign *alter* (change), *faucet* (spigot or tap), *gawk* (stare), and *flawless* (perfect) to students to look up in a grade-appropriate dictionary and ask them to report back to the group.

Sorting and Discussion:

1. Read the words quickly and discuss any that might be unfamiliar or that may have multiple meanings. Ask, **What do you notice about this collection of words?** Probe with, **What syllables are accented?** (The first syllable.) **What vowel sounds do you hear? How could we sort these words?** Accept different possibilities. Students should be able to sort the words independently by the vowel pattern headers, but remind them to watch out for some oddballs.

2. After sorting, read down each column emphasizing the first syllable. Ask, **What are the oddballs and why?** (*Laughed* has a short *a* sound. *Allow* does not have the /al/ sound in the first syllable but has the -*ow* pattern in the final syllable that was covered in the previous sort.)

3. Ask, **What can we conclude from this sort to help you as readers and spellers?** Looking for the *au*, *aw*, and *al* patterns can help readers decode unfamiliar words, but there are no clues for spellers.

Extend: Assign standard weekly routines. At some point, draw students' attention to some other features of the words. Ask, **Can you find some words that have a silent consonant that could make a word hard to spell?** (*autumn, although*) **What word must be capitalized and why?** (*August*) **What words have a base word that can help you spell the words?** (*flawless, although, laughed*, etc.)

Apply: Display some unfamiliar words from the list below for students to read and spell. Talk about their choices and how breaking the word into syllables can help. The speller can hear the /ô/ sound, but with three patterns, it is hard to know which one is correct. Is it *gaudy, galdy,* or *gawdy*? It is important to learn which pattern goes with a word, and a dictionary is needed for unfamiliar words.

Additional Words: *cauldron, gaudy, jaunty, haunches, trauma, pauper, cautious, awfully, gnawed, lawless, tawny, yawning, brawny, walrus, altar, almost, altogether, already, halter, falter, waltz;* oddballs: *drawer, wallet.*

SORT 25   *AU, AW*, and *AL* in Accented Syllables

au	*aw*	*al*
saucer	**awful**	**also**
always	author	salty
August	alter	lawyer
although	awkward	autumn
laundry	laughed	awesome
allow	caution	flawless
faucet	walnut	auction
gawking	sausage	haunted

Sort 26   R-Influenced A in Accented Syllables

Generalization: Familiar r-influenced vowel patterns (ar, air, are) show up in two-syllable words and can be clearly heard in the accented syllable. A new pattern is a followed by double r (arr).

ar	air	are	arr
garden	**airplane**	**careful**	**carry***
market	haircut	parents	narrow
carpet	dairy	prepare	carrot
harvest	fairy	barely	marry
tardy	unfair	beware	
hardly		aware	
partner			
pardon			
barber			

Sorting and Discussion:

1. Display the words without showing the pattern headers. Read the words quickly and discuss any that might be unfamiliar. Ask, **What do you notice about this collection of words?** Students should notice the familiar patterns. **What vowel sounds do you hear? Do you hear a long a in airplane or compare?** Most would agree they do. Talk about how the vowels are r-influenced or r-controlled, and give examples that contrast short a and with r-influenced a (e.g., bat/bar) and long a with are and air (ate/air).
2. **How could we sort these words? What are familiar patterns? What is a new pattern?** (arr) Students should be able to sort the words independently by the pattern headers.
3. After sorting, read through the words emphasizing the stressed syllable. Ask, **Where does the accent usually fall?** (The first syllable.) **Can we find some words under the are pattern that are accented on the second syllable?** (beware, aware, and prepare) Explain, **The sound of the vowel in the unaccented first syllable of these words is not very clear, and you will need to remember it.** Recall words such as annoy and about from earlier sorts. Talk about how sometimes spellers accent the syllable to help them identify the vowel (saying bē' ware or prē' pare) but not when they speak normally.
4. Ask, **What can we conclude from this sort to help you as readers and spellers?** Looking for the ar, air, and are patterns can help students read unfamiliar words. Keep those patterns in mind as they spell words.

Extend: Use the standard weekly routines. Ask, **Can you find some compound words in this sort?** (airplane, haircut) **Is carpet a compound word? Why or why not?** (While it is made up of two smaller words, the meaning of the compound word is not related to either of the two smaller words.)

Apply: Select some less familiar words from the list below to practice decoding. Talk about likely places to break the words into syllables, but accept approximations. Ask students to spell a word such as cartoon or airport and talk about how they decided to spell the first syllable. The /är/ sound is nearly always spelled with ar, and thinking of a base word can help spell the others.

Additional Words: artist, party, parka, larva, garlic, margin, bargain, carbon, scarlet, sparkle, target, harbor, carton, cartoon, barefoot, stairway, fairway, airport, chairman, prairie, impair, affair, airfare, hardware, nightmare, software, parrot, sparrow, narrate, barrel.

SORT 26   *R*-Influenced *A* in Accented Syllables

ar	*air*	*are*	*arr*
garden	**airplane**	**careful**	
carry	market	aware	
carpet	narrow	parents	
tardy	haircut	harvest	
unfair	prepare	carrot	
fairy	hardly	marry	
partner	beware	pardon	
barber	barely	dairy	

Sort 27   R-Influenced O in Accented Syllables

Generalization: Familiar *r*-influenced *o* patterns (*or*, *ore*) show up in two-syllable words and can be clearly heard in the accented syllable. The *or* pattern is much more common than *ore*.

or	ore	oddball
morning*	before*	fourteen
order*	ashore	sorry
shorter	explore	
forest	ignore	
corner	adore	
inform		
forty		
northern		
border		
orbit		
chorus		
florist		
record		
perform		
report		
horrid		
stormy		

Explore Meaning: *Ashore* may not be familiar, but using it in a sentence such as *A shell washed ashore* is probably enough to establish the meaning. *Horrid* can be compared to *horrible*. *Record* is a homograph with two pronunciations and meanings. It will be explored further in Sort 57.

Sorting and Discussion:

1. Display the words without the pattern headers. Read the words quickly and discuss any that might be unfamiliar. Ask, **What do you notice about this collection of words?** Review the term r-*influenced* with examples of words such as *for* or *more*. Probe with, **What syllables are accented?** (The first and last.) **What vowel sounds do you hear? How could we sort these words?** Accept different possibilities, and display the headers for *or* and *ore*.

2. Explain, **Let's sort first by the r-influenced vowel patterns.** Students should be able to sort the words independently using the headers, but remind them to watch out for some oddballs.

3. After sorting, read down each column, emphasizing the accented syllable. Ask, **What do you notice about the words in each column? Where**

do you see the *ore* pattern? (At the end of a two-syllable word.) **Which pattern do you think might be most common? Let's see which one turns up more in a word hunt. What are the oddballs and why?** *Sorry* does not have the /or/ sound. Compare *forty* and *fourteen*. *Fourteen* is not really an oddball because there are other words with the *our* pattern (*your*, *court*, *pour*), but there is no place for it in this sort. Remind students of how most -*teen* words just add the ending to a base word, and ask if they remember which ones do not (*thirteen*, *fifteen*).

4. If time allows, challenge students to sort by accented syllables. Ask, **Where do you see the *ore* pattern?** (In the second accented syllable—similar to an open syllable.) **Where do you see *or*?** (Followed by a consonant.) *Fourteen* might be an oddball because both syllables seem to get equal stress.

5. Ask, **What can we conclude from this sort to help you as readers and spellers?** Looking for the *or* and *ore* patterns can help students read unfamiliar words. *Or* is the most common spelling for the ôr sound, but *ore* comes at the end of accented second syllables.

1st		2nd		oddball
morning*	forty	before*	ignore	fourteen
shorter	northern	record	adore	sorry
order*	border	perform	inform	
forest	orbit	ashore		
corner	chorus	report		
horrid	florist	explore		
stormy				

Extend: Complete standard weekly routines. Combine and list the words students find in a word hunt to confirm if the pattern *or* is more common. You might draw students' attention to the first sound in *chorus*, which has the sound of hard *c* rather than the more familiar /ch/. Assess by calling at least 10 words aloud for students to spell.

Apply: Display some unfamiliar words from the list below, and guide students to break the words into syllables before decoding. Call aloud a few words like *hornet* and *restore* and talk about the choices for spelling. *Or* is the most frequent spelling of the /ôr/ sound—except when it is the final sound in the second accented syllable.

Additional Words: *torment, fortress, tortoise, portrait, boring, corncob, orchard, horrid, hornet, normal, forward, organ, morsel, restore, galore, afford, reform, distort, endorse, import.*

SORT 27   *R*-Influenced *O* in Accented Syllables

or	*ore*	*oddball*
morning	**before**	order
record	shorter	perform
forest	sorry	fourteen
horrid	corner	ashore
forty	report	northern
explore	border	stormy
orbit	chorus	ignore
adore	florist	inform

Sort 28   Words with the *W* or */W/* Sound Before the Vowel

While the *r* is well known for influencing the vowels that follow it, this is also true for *w*. The sound of *w* (sometimes spelled with *u* as in *quarter* or *squad*) changes the *ar* in *warmth* to /or/ and the *or* in *worker* to /er/. What would normally be a short *a* in a CVC word like *watch* is instead the broad *a* sound of /ah/ or /ä/.

Generalization: The sound of *a*, *ar*, and *or* often changes after *w* or the /w/ sound in *qu*.

war	wor	wa
warmth	worker	watch
wardrobe	worse	swallow
warning	world	wander
warden	worry	water
quarter	worthy	squash
warrior	worship	wallet
toward		squad
quarrel		
swarm		
dwarf		
backward		

Explore Meaning: *Quarter* can refer to a coin that is one-fourth of a dollar or simply one-fourth. Relate *wardrobe* to the book and movie *The Lion, the Witch, and the Wardrobe* and talk about its meanings (a stand-alone closet but also a collection of clothes). Compare *wonder* (to question or to be curious) and *wander* (to move from place to place without direction) to be sure students have the correct meaning. They might add a question mark to the word card for *wonder*.

Sorting and Discussion:

1. Display the words without the headers. Read the words quickly and discuss any that might be unfamiliar. Ask, **What do you notice about this collection of words?** Take multiple responses, but if needed probe with, **What happens to *a* after *w*? What happens to the *ar* pattern? To the *or* pattern?** Ask, **Do you recall learning about this in one-syllable words like *war* and *word*?**
2. **How could we sort these words?** Take different ideas, but explain, **Let's sort first by vowel patterns using the headers *war*, *wor*, and *wa*.** Students should be able to sort the words independently by the vowel pattern headers, but remind them to watch out for some oddballs. Words with *qu* can go into oddballs for now.
3. After sorting, read down each column and ask, **How are these words alike? What are the oddballs and why? What do you notice about the *u* in *quarter* and *quarrel*?** (It has the /w/ sound.) **What about in words like *squad* and *squash*?** Explain, **In these words the *u* has the *w* sound, so let's move them under the headers with the same vowel sound.**
4. Ask students to sort again, listening carefully to the vowel sounds so that words with *qu* end up in the correct categories.

Extend: Complete the standard weekly routines. It may be difficult to find more words with these patterns, but accept one-syllable words in word hunts. Students can look for other words that begin with *w* (such as *window* or *weekend*) in which the vowel after the *w* is not influenced by it. This will help them see that this influence is limited to words that begin with *wa* or *wo*.

Ward is a base word that occurs in many compound words suggesting direction, such as *toward* and *backward*. Simply point in different directions to help elicit many of them from students: *inward, outward, forward, backward, downward, upward.*

Apply: Select words from below for students to read and spell. Listening for base words will help them spell words like *backward* or *westward*.

Additional Words: *reward, toward, inward, outward, forward, backward, downward, upward, skyward, westward, eastward, worthwhile, squalid, swaddle, waddle, wallow, squabble, waffle;* oddball: *coward.*

SORT 28   Words with the *W* or */W/* Sound Before the Vowel

war	*wor*	*wa*
warmth	**worker**	**watch**
quarter	wardrobe	worse
world	water	warden
warning	worry	squad
toward	warrior	worthy
quarrel	worship	swarm
swallow	dwarf	wallet
squash	wander	backward

Sort 29   *ER*, *IR*, and *UR* in Accented Syllables

Generalization: The *er*, *ir*, and *ur* patterns spell the /ûr/ sound in two-syllable words and can be clearly heard in the accented syllable.

er	ir	ur	oddball
person	**thirty**	**sturdy**	spirit
nervous	firmly	hurry	every*
perfect	dirty	further	
hermit	birthday	purple	
mermaid	thirsty	turtle	
serpent	birdbath	furnish	
	circus	burger	
		during	
		Thursday	

Explore Meaning: *Hermit* (one who lives alone) and *furnish* (provide or put furniture into) may not be familiar, so have students look them up.

Sorting and Discussion:

1. Display the words without the pattern headers. Read the words quickly and discuss any that might be unfamiliar. Ask, **What do you notice about this collection of words?** Probe with, **What syllables are accented?** (The first syllable.) **What vowel sound do you hear? How could we sort these words?** Accept different possibilities and display the pattern headers.
2. Explain, **Let's sort first by the *r*-influenced vowel patterns.** Students should be able to sort the words independently using the headers, but remind them to watch out for some oddballs.
3. After sorting, read down each column, emphasizing the accented syllable. (Note that *perhaps* is accented on the second syllable. Compound words like *birdbath* have somewhat equal stress.) Ask, **What are the oddballs and why?** In *spirit*, the *ir* pattern does not have the /ûr/ sound. Ask students how to pronounce *every*. (ev-rē) Most say it as a two-syllable word and /ûr/ is missing. However, it helps when spelling this common word to pronounce it as a three-syllable word: /ev-ûr-ē/. Some students might put *hurry* as an oddball because it has the *urr* pattern. Accept it in either place.
4. **What can we conclude from this sort?** The /ûr/ sound can be spelled in at least three different ways (*er*, *ir*, *ur*). **Can someone think of another way to spell the /ûr/ sound?** (*ear* as in *earth*)

Extend: Assign standard routines for linking to text and writing. Accept words in a word hunt that are accented in either syllable (e.g., *perhaps*). Call aloud at least 10 words for a weekly assessment.

Apply: Select some less familiar words from the list below (*sherbet*, *whirlpool*, *murmur*, etc.). Break them into syllables with student help and read them. Compare *thirty* and *thirteen* and how these words differs from *forty* and *fourteen*.

Additional Words: *perhaps, mercy, sermon, thermos kernel, gerbil, sherbet, certain, merchant, version, servant, verdict, service, thirteen, virtue, skirmish, circuit, irksome, whirlpool, chirping, mural, purpose, surfer, burden, curfew, hurdle, jury, murmur, turnip, burner, murder, surplus, curtain.*

SORT 29   *ER*, *IR*, and *UR* in Accented Syllables

er	*ir*	*ur*
person	**thirty**	**sturdy**
firmly	nervous	burger
perfect	further	dirty
hurry	birthday	circus
spirit	mermaid	Thursday
hermit	turtle	thirsty
birdbath	serpent	furnish
during	every	purple

Sort 30   *URE*, *EAR*, and *ERE* in Accented Syllables

This is a somewhat complicated sort with a number of unfamiliar words, so we recommend starting with a teacher-directed sound sort. There are fewer words in this challenging sort.

Generalization: The /ûr/ sound can also be spelled with the *ear* and *ure* patterns. The *ear* pattern also spells /ēr/ along with *ere* and *eer*.

ure = ur	*ear* = ur	*ēar*	*ēre*	oddball
secure	early*	nearby	severe	cheerful
mature	earthquake	teardrop	sincere	
endure	learner	spearmint	adhere	
insure	earnest	weary		
	rehearse	appear		
	yearning	dreary		
		nearly		

Explore Meaning: Words to look up and discuss as unfamiliar include *insure* (guard against loss), *endure* (stick with something), *earnest* (serious), *yearning* (longing for), *dreary* (gloomy), *adhere* (stick), and *weary* (very tired). Present words in phrases such as "insure the car, endure pain, earnest effort, yearning for a pet, dreary day, adhere to a schedule, and feeling weary."

Sorting and Discussion:

1. Display the words without the pattern headers. Read the words quickly and take time to discuss any that might be unfamiliar. Ask, **What do you notice about this collection of words?** Probe with, **What syllables are accented?** (The first and last.) **What vowel sounds do you hear? How could we sort these words?** Accept different possibilities, but start with a sound sort. Create your own sound headers (/ur/ and /ēr/), model sorting one in each category, and then sort the rest with student help.

2. After sorting by sound, read down each column, emphasizing the sound in the accented syllable. Then ask, **What patterns do you see for each sound? How can we sort again?** Display the pattern headers and sort each column by patterns as shown. **What is the oddball?** (cheerful)

3. **What can we conclude from this sort?** Probe with, **What patterns did we find last week for the /ûr/ sound?** (*er, ir, ur*) **What pattern can we add to those?** (*ure, ear*) **How do we spell the /ēr/ sound?** (*ear, ere*) **Think about position. Where does the *ure* pattern come? The *ere* pattern?** (At the end of words.) **Which words have a base word?** (*learner, nearby, spearmint*, etc.) **How can that help you spell or read the word?**

4. Ask students to sort again by pattern and sound under your supervision if time allows.

Extend: During weekly routines, ask students to sort by the pattern headers each time. Revisit word meanings on other days, perhaps putting words in phrases or composing sentences together. You might supply some sentence starters like the following:

> I am very earnest about _____.
> I am yearning for _____.
> _____ can adhere to paper.
> It was a dreary day because _____.
> I was feeling weary after _____.

Apply: Select some words from the list below. With student help, break them into syllables to read.

Additional Words: *assure, impure, brochure, azure, demure, ensure, earnings, pearly, yearbook, earthworm, research, clearing, dearest, earache, bleary, nearly, earring, endear, cashmere, revere, cheerful, career, eerie.*

SORT 30   *URE*, *EAR*, and *ERE* in Accented Syllables

ure = ur	*ear* = ur	*ēre*	*ēar*
secure	**early**	**nearby**	
severe	nearly	earthquake	
spearmint	mature	teardrop	
earnest	endure	insure	
sincere	weary	learner	
rehearse	appear	yearning	
adhere	dreary	cheerful	

UNIT REVIEW AND ASSESSMENT

Review:

The sound of /ûr/ can be spelled in many ways including *er, ir, ur, ure, wor,* and *ear*. This makes it a particularly challenging sound to spell. Ask students to go through their word study notebooks to find all the words with the sound and list them by pattern.

You may also want to make a group list of all the words that students were able to find as a guide to which pattern is most frequent. Games such as *Match* or *Memory*, described in *Words Their Way*, are simple games to review these words before the posttest.

Assess:

To check for retention of the words in this unit, administer the unit spell check found on page 80.

Unit VI   Unaccented Syllables

NOTES FOR THE TEACHER

Background and Objectives

In previous units, the feature of attention was familiar vowel patterns in the accented syllable. Now we turn our attention to the unaccented syllable in which the vowel sound is often the *schwa* sound /ə/, as in the first syllable of *about*, or the final sound in *table* or *nickel*. These unaccented syllables are challenging to spell because sound is not a useful clue when the same sound is spelled several different ways. (Is it *nickel*, *nickle*, or *nickal*?) While the spelling of some words simply has to be memorized, these sorts will show that some spellings are much more likely than others, which can lead to a "best guess" strategy. For example, the ending -*le* is far more common than the endings -*el*, -*il*, or -*al*, and -*er* is much more common than -*or* or -*ar*. Students will also learn that comparative adjectives (*bigger*, *better*) are always spelled with -*er*. During this unit students will:

- Identify the unaccented syllable and learn the appropriate spelling patterns
- Know when to change the *y* to *i* before -*ed* and -*s*
- Spell the words in these sorts correctly

Targeted Learners

These sorts are designed for students in the middle syllable and affixes stage who are making errors such as BOTTEL for *bottle*, FAVER for *favor*, and RIPIN for *ripen*. Unit Spell Check 6 can be used as a pretest to assess more thoroughly the features covered in these sorts. Students who score 90% or better can move on to other sorts.

Teaching Tips

The standard weekly routines described on pages 6–8 are important for the extra practice and extensions they offer. Word hunts in daily reading materials will turn up additional words for most of these sorts and will help students develop a sense of the frequency of certain final unaccented syllable spellings. You may want to create group lists of all the words students find for each category to enhance these discoveries; these can be reviewed at the end to reinforce the role of frequency when using a "best guess" spelling strategy.

If you teach *syllable types*, this unit covers the last of the six types: final stable syllables. This includes the common "consonant-*le*" pattern (*table*, *cycle*, *buckle*) as well as other final unaccented syllables (*nation*, *creature*, *label*).

Create games and activities such as those in Chapters 6 and 7 of *Words Their Way*. *Apple and Bushel* in Chapter 7 will work well for words that end in -*el* and -*le* and can be adapted for other unaccented syllables. *Dinosaur Take-a-Card* (for -*el*, -*le*, -*il*, and -*al*) and *Feed the Alligator* (for -*an*, -*in*, -*on*, and -*ain*) can be downloaded ready to use from the online PDToolkit. These games can be adapted for other endings.

Some of the words in these sorts may not be well known, so we urge you to discuss their meanings during the introduction and follow up with more discussion later in the week. Suggestions are given in the sorts that follow about particular words and the use of the dictionary. You may want students to look up the meanings of some words to add to the discussion before or after the initial sort.

Comparing cognates may help English learners to attend to pronunciation. For example, the word *valley* is spelled the same in English and Spanish but is accented differently in Spanish. Students should be encouraged to find the meaning connections across languages as in the Spanish word for *goalie: el portero* can mean both "goalie" as well as "doorman." English speakers can broaden their vocabulary knowledge by considering the cognates and then the related words in English, but all students can benefit from these discussions. For example, the Spanish word for *bargain* is *negociar*, which is related to the word *negotiate* in English—to obtain a bargain, one might need to negotiate.

UNIT SPELL CHECK 6 ASSESSMENT FOR UNACCENTED SYLLABLES

Call the words aloud for students to spell on a sheet of notebook paper. Use in sentences if necessary to clarify meaning.

1. carried	**2.** capture	**3.** model
4. gallon	**5.** afraid	**6.** valley
7. measure	**8.** title	**9.** eleven
10. April	**11.** signal	**12.** dollar
13. degree	**14.** younger	**15.** copying
16. movie	**17.** napkin	**18.** because
19. tutor	**20.** weather	

Interpreting Scores on Pre- and Posttests

Use the goal setting form on page 4 to analyze and record results and the pacing guide on page 5 to plan which sorts to use.

- **90% or better**—Students can move on to the next unit.
- **75% to 85%**—A "gray area" where teacher judgment is needed. Examine the types of errors students make to see if there are particular features that can be targeted rather than doing all the sorts.
- **70% or less**—Students will benefit from doing all the sorts in the unit.

Sort 31   Unaccented Final Syllable (-*LE*)

This sort reviews syllable juncture patterns as it introduces unaccented syllables. It is optional because the -*le* ending is covered in the next sort as well. This is a new unit with a new focus, so you may want to begin with a teacher-directed sort.

Generalization: The pattern -*le* often comes at the end of a word and is unaccented.

VCle	VCCle doublet	VCCle
title	little*	simple
cradle	middle	tremble
able	settle	single
table	bottle	tickle
rifle	apple	sample
maple	puddle	jungle
bugle	giggle	handle
cable	battle	candle

*High-frequency word

Explore Meaning: The word *cable* has several different meanings. It can be a chain, rope, or bundle of wires. Talk briefly about what it means to have cable television—a cable brings sound and images into the house. *Maple* is a kind of tree but also a flavor. Students may have heard of maple syrup.

Sorting and Discussion:

1. Review syllable patterns if you think it is needed. Write the words *super*, *butter*, and *basket* and remind students of the syllable juncture patterns they assigned to these words: VCV and VCCV (with and without doublets). Underline the corresponding letters in the words, as in the *u, p,* and *e* of the VCV pattern in *super*. Explain, **You will be reviewing juncture patterns in the words for this week.**
2. Prepare a set of words to use for teacher-directed modeling and set aside the headers. Read the words quickly, and discuss any that might be unfamiliar. Ask, **What do you notice about this collection of words?** Talk about how they are all two syllables and all end with -*le*. Ask, **How could we sort these words?** Accept different possibilities, but agree to sort by the syllable patterns using the headers provided with the sort. Put up the headers and key words (*title, little,* and *simple*), and point out the syllable juncture pattern that precedes the ending of -*le*. Explain, **The -*le* is always connected to a**

consonant, and the syllable juncture patterns are modified to reflect this. For example, VCV is now represented as VCle.** Sort the rest of the words with student help.
3. After sorting, say, **Read these words with me and pay attention to where we put the accent.** Sometimes students can "feel" the stress if they gently place the top of their hand under their chin as they say the words. **What do you notice about the accent or stress?** (It is on the first syllable in all the words.) Explain, **We say that the last syllable is the "unaccented" syllable. What is the sound you hear in that unaccented syllable?** (/əl/)
4. Talk about each column in turn. **What can you say about the words in each column? How are they alike?** Talk about the sound of the vowel in the first syllable, whether it is open or closed, and where the word would be split into syllables. Probe as needed with questions such as **Which words have open syllables? When is the vowel long?**
5. Ask, **What can we learn from this sort to help you as readers and spellers?** Talk about how many words end in -*le*.

Extend: See the list of standard weekly routines for follow-up activities to the basic sorting lesson on pages 6–8. Word hunts will turn up lots of words that end in -*le*, including some that will have a different vowel pattern associated with a familiar syllable juncture pattern (such as *double*), which can go in an oddball category. Call aloud at least 10 words for a weekly assessment.

Students might be directed to the dictionary to look up several words and see how the final syllable is represented in the pronunciation guide for the word. Explain that the upside-down *e* is called a *schwa* sound.

Apply: Select some words from the list below that are probably unfamiliar and ask students to read them (e.g., *noble, muffle, twinkle*). Ask, **What can help you read these words?** (Look for familiar vowel patterns in the first syllable.) Ask them to spell some words that you call aloud from the list (*fable, paddle, scramble*) and ask, **What can help you spell these words?** Listening for the vowel sound is a clue when deciding whether to double or not.

Additional Words: *idle, noble, cycle, bridle, Bible, rattle, paddle, wriggle, pebble, scribble, juggle, muffle, struggle, bubble, puzzle, fiddle, scramble, sprinkle, twinkle, crackle, mumble, bundle, tangle, muscle.*

SORT 31   Unaccented Final Syllable (-*LE*)

VCle	VCCle doublet	VCCle
title	**little**	**simple**
middle	able	tremble
cable	single	settle
bottle	table	tickle
cradle	apple	puddle
giggle	jungle	maple
bugle	battle	handle
candle	sample	rifle

Sort 32   Unaccented Final Syllable (-LE, -EL, -IL, -AL)

Generalization: The sound of the final syllable /əl/ can be spelled several ways, but is most commonly spelled -le.

-le	-el	-il	-al	oddball
cattle	**model**	**pencil**	**final**	
pebble	level	April	total	special
marble	angel	fossil	metal	until*
angle	novel	evil	signal	
	nickel		local	
	vowel		journal	
	travel		oval	

Explore Meaning: *Novel* has two meanings to discuss (a book or something new). *Marble* refers to a kind of stone used for building as well as a small round ball. Speculate about how marbles might have been made of round stones, or *pebbles*, at one time.

Sorting and Discussion:

1. You may want to introduce this sort with a short spelling test. Ask students to spell *cattle, model, pencil,* and *final.* Talk about what makes the words hard to spell. (They all have the same /əl/ sound in the final unaccented syllable.)

2. Display the words in the sort without showing the headers. Read over them quickly and talk about any that students might not know. Ask, **What do you notice about all the words?** Review the term *final unaccented syllable* and how the words all end with the same sound. Ask, **How can we sort these words?** Students might suggest different things such as the pattern in the middle or stress. Display the headers and let students sort independently by the final syllable. Warn them, **Watch out for some oddballs.** (They are not easy to find in this sort.)

3. After sorting, read the words in each column and emphasize the accented syllable. This is where students might find out that *until* is accented on a different syllable. Ask, **What can we say about the vowel in the accented syllable?** (It is usually easy to hear as long or short.) **What about the sound in the unaccented syllable?** (It just sounds like /uhl/ or /əl/ and is called the *schwa* plus *l* sound.) **What makes it hard to spell the *schwa* plus *l* sound?** (It has

four different patterns.) **What is the oddball and why?** Students may have put *special* with the other words ending in -al, but ask how it is different. (It ends in -ial.) *Until* looks like it goes with the other -il words, but it is accented on the second syllable and the vowel in the final syllable sounds like short *i* not /əl/.

4. **What will make the words for this week hard to spell?** Students will have to memorize which final pattern to use with each word because sound is not a clue in the second syllable. *Angle* and *angel* are often confused, but the sound of the *g* is a clue. Point out how the *g* in *angel* is "softened" by the following *e* but remains hard before the *l* in *angle.* Pose the question, **Remember how we had a lot of -le words last week. I wonder if one of these patterns is more common than the others?**

5. Ask students to sort again if time allows, and remind them to watch for the oddballs.

Extend: Use standard weekly routines. A word hunt will be very useful with this sort to reveal the frequencies of patterns. Although the -le column is quite short here, it is by far the most common spelling and will turn up in word hunts with the greatest frequency. Words spelled with -el are not too rare, but students will find it challenging to find more words for the -il and -al categories. Bring students together to compile a list of all the words they found to emphasize the most common patterns. Add words from last week as well.

Apple and Bushel, described in Chapter 7 of *Words Their Way,* is designed to differentiate between -el and -le endings and can be adapted to include -il and -al as well. *Dinosaur Take-a-Card,* available at the PDToolkit, reviews all four.

Apply: After reviewing the results of a word hunt, ask students to form a "best guess" strategy if they hear the sound in a word that they are not sure how to spell. How would they likely spell the name *Mable*? Or the word *frindle*? (*Frindle* is the name of a book by Andrew Clements in which a boy decides to invent a new word and, of course, has to invent a spelling for it also.)

Additional Words: *saddle, dimple, tingle, freckle, huddle, kennel, label, towel, shovel, channel, camel, cancel, gravel, peril, tonsil, pupil, civil, council, scandal, neutral, crystal, global, medal, tidal, plural, fertile, hostile.*

SORT 32   Unaccented Final Syllable (-*LE*, -*EL*, -*IL*, -*AL*)

-le	*-el*	*-al*	*-il*
cattle	**model**		**final**
pencil	level		April
total	marble		angel
novel	fossil		metal
pebble	nickel		oval
travel	special		vowel
signal	journal		angle
evil	until		local

Sort 33   Unaccented Final Syllable (-ER, -OR, -AR)

It is not always easy to determine where the syllable break comes in these words. Sometimes the /ər/ stands alone, as in *col-or* or *weath-er*, and sometimes it is attached to a consonant, as in *sis-ter* or *sil-ver*. Don't expect students to master syllable breaks, but generally looking for open syllables (as in *fa-vor* and *spi-der*) and closed syllables (as in *sil-ver* and *col-lar*) will be close enough to help students focus attention on unaccented syllables and their spellings.

Generalization: The sound of the final syllable /ər/ can be spelled several ways, but it is most commonly spelled *-er*.

-er	-or	-ar
other*	color*	dollar
mother*	doctor	collar
weather	favor	solar
sister	error	sugar
silver	mirror	grammar
under*	motor	
father	rumor	
flower	tractor	
spider	harbor	
brother		

Explore Meaning: Talk about the meaning of the word *solar* (having to do with the sun) and ask for examples such as *solar power, solar panels, solar eclipse,* and so on. The word *harbor* can be a noun (e.g., a body of water where boats seek shelter) or a verb (e.g., to keep thoughts or feelings in one's mind, as in to harbor a grudge).

Sorting and Discussion:

1. You may want to introduce this with a short spelling test. Ask students to spell *other, color,* and *dollar.* Talk about what makes the words hard to spell. (They all have the same /ər/ sound in the final unaccented syllable.)
2. Read the words without showing the headers, and talk about any that students might not know. Ask, **What do you notice about all the words?** Review the term *final unaccented syllable* and how the words all end with the same sound of /ər/. Ask, **How can we sort these words?** Students might suggest different things such as the pattern in the middle or stress. Display the headers and let students sort independently by the final syllable.

3. After sorting, read the words in each column and emphasize the accented syllable. Ask, **What can we say about the sound in the unaccented syllable?** (It sounds like /ər/.)
4. **What will make the words for this week hard to spell?** (The /ər/ sound can be spelled with three different patterns.) Students will have to memorize which final pattern to use with each word because sound is not a clue in the second syllable. Pose the question, **Remember how we found last week that -le was the most common pattern? I wonder if one of these patterns is more common than the others? What do you think it would be?**
5. You may want to extend students' understanding with, **Sometimes a spelling clue can be provided by a word that is related in meaning to a hard-to-spell word.** Write the word *grammar* and then *grammatical* directly beneath it. **When we say a sentence is *grammatical*, what does that mean? When you look at the word *grammatical*, can you find a clue that will help you spell *grammar*?** If students are unsure, underline the *a* in the second syllables of *grammar* and *grammatical*. **Can you hear how the second syllable in *grammatical* is stressed? What vowel sound do you hear in that syllable? Right, a short *a*. Because these two words are similar in meaning, thinking of that accented short *a* in *grammatical* will help you spell the unaccented /ər/ syllable in *grammar*.** Occasionally "mentioning" these types of spelling–meaning connections will set the stage for deeper, more focused exploration in the derivational relations stage.

Extend: Use a word hunt to answer the question of frequency, and compile a group list of all the words students can find. Again, have students use the dictionary to check how the unaccented syllable is represented in the pronunciation guide. Call at least 10 words aloud for a weekly spelling test.

Apply: After reviewing the results of the word hunt, ask students what their best guess would be for spelling a word like *ranger* or *crater*. What would they need to do to be sure? Look it up! Display the words *solar, lunar,* and *polar* and ask how they are related. They all might be used in a study of space and they all end in *-ar*.

Additional Words: *stranger, cover, danger, rather, center, proper, roller, rubber, crater, printer, fiber, liter, litter, lumber, manner, horror, razor, splendor, terror, tremor, vapor, tumor, error, cedar, cheddar, lunar, molar, polar, nectar, liar.*

SORT 33   Unaccented Final Syllable (-*ER*, -*OR*, -*AR*)

-*er*	-*or*	-*ar*
other	**color**	**dollar**
doctor	spider	sugar
brother	collar	favor
solar	sister	silver
weather	error	mother
flower	father	mirror
under	rumor	motor
tractor	grammar	harbor

Sort 34   Agents and Comparatives

Generalization: Comparative adjectives (*bigger*, *smaller*) are always spelled with *-er*. Agents are spelled with *-er*, *-ar*, and *-or*, but *-er* is most common.

people who do things			words that compare
dancer	actor	beggar	bigger
dreamer	sailor	burglar	faster
driver	traitor		longer
farmer	tutor		smaller
jogger			fresher
writer			younger
shopper			older
swimmer			smoother
voter			brighter

Explore Meaning: The word *traitor* (someone who is unfaithful, who turns against you) may not be familiar, so ask someone to look it up.

Sorting and Discussion:

1. Without showing the headers, read through these words and talk about any that might be unfamiliar. Ask, **What do you notice about these words?** Take different ideas before prompting, **Can you find words that name people who do things?** Explain that such people might be called agents. Ask, **What do you notice about the other words? What do words like *bigger* and *older* do?** (They describe things.) Explain, **These words are called *comparative adjectives* because they compare two things. For example, *An elephant is bigger than a horse.***

2. Introduce the two headers and sort as a group, or ask students to sort independently. After sorting, ask, **Can we sort these words another way?** Use the key words to head subcategories and sort the words further by the spelling of the final unaccented syllable. Ask, **What do you notice about comparative adjectives?** (They are all spelled with *-er*.) **What about agents or people who do things?** (Sometimes they end in *-or* or *-ar*, but usually they end in *-er*.) Remind students of what they learned in the last sort: The *-er* pattern is the most common.

3. Review the rules for adding endings on a second day. Write the words *beg*, *begging*, *begged*, and *beggar*. Ask, **What do you notice about adding endings to the base word *beg*?** Review the rules students learned about adding *-ed* and *-ing* to words with VC at the end. Explain that similar rules apply when adding *-er*, *-ar*, or *-or* to a base word because the endings start with a vowel.

4. *Traitor*, *tutor*, and *burglar* do not have base words, so turn them over and write the headers "double," "*e*-drop," and "nothing" on the back to use for the next sort. Ask the students to sort the words according to the rule as shown below. Have them add this sort to their word study notebooks.

double	e-drop	nothing	
beggar	driver	dreamer	older
jogger	writer	farmer	smoother
swimmer	dancer	sailor	brighter
bigger	voter	younger	longer
shopper		smaller	fresher
		faster	actor

Extend: Use standard weekly routines. During a word hunt, students should look for more agents and comparatives and see if they can reach some conclusions about the most common spellings. Help students write a conclusion about when to use *-er*.

Because comparatives include a lot of antonyms, you might challenge students to match pairs such as *older–younger* and *bigger–smaller*, and to come up with antonyms for *smoother*, *faster*, *longer*, and *brighter*. More pairs can be found among the additional words below.

Apply: Ask students to spell *cooler*, *hotter*, *diver*, and *catcher* and to justify their spellings by talking about the rules for adding endings and the best bet for choosing which way to spell the ending.

Additional Words: *speaker, skater, racer, tailor, donor, scholar, dimmer, shorter, smarter, braver, cheaper, weaker, stronger, quicker, slower, lighter, darker, tamer, wilder, hotter, cooler, richer, poorer, diver, catcher.*

SORT 34   Agents and Comparatives

people who do things	words that compare	
dancer	**bigger**	**actor**
beggar	dreamer	faster
longer	smaller	driver
farmer	burglar	traitor
fresher	jogger	younger
writer	older	sailor
smoother	swimmer	brighter
tutor	shopper	voter

Sort 35   Unaccented Final Syllables (/CHUR/ and /ZHUR/)

The unaccented final syllables in these words have two spellings (-er and -ure) and several sounds that are similar but subtly different. Although we ask students to sort by the sounds, do not be overly concerned if there is disagreement and inconsistency. The point is not as much to sort the words correctly by sound as it is to see that the words are spelled with the same pattern (-ure) despite these slight differences.

Generalization: The /ər/ (or /ur/) sound in the unaccented final syllable preceded by *ch, t*, or *s* sounds like /chur/ or/zhur/.

-cher = /chur/	-ture = /chur/	-sure = /zhur/	oddball
catcher	picture	measure	senior
rancher	nature	treasure	figure
teacher	capture	pleasure	failure
pitcher	future	leisure	
stretcher	mixture		
butcher	creature		
	moisture		
	posture		
	torture		
	culture		
	injure		

Explore Meaning: *Figure* refers to "form or shape" (noun) but can also mean to "consider" (verb) as in *figure something out. Leisure* (time of rest) has two pronunciations (lē' zhər or leh' zhər). Share these with students as an opportunity to show how pronunciation differs and how to use a pronunciation guide in the dictionary.

Sorting and Discussion:

1. Because this is challenging, use a teacher-directed sort. Read the words quickly, and talk about any that might be unfamiliar. If students struggle to read any of the words, set them aside to revisit later. Ask, **What do you notice about these words?** Take multiple responses. Review, **We have sorted words before ending in the /ər/ sound. What patterns have we studied to spell these sounds?** (-er, -ar, -or) **Do you see another pattern in these words?** (-ure) Listen to the sound in *catcher*. **Do you hear just**

/ər/ at the end or a slightly different sound? (/chur/) **What about at the end of *picture*? The end of *measure*?**

2. Display the headers and explain, **The spelling pattern is at the top of each header. The slash marks below indicate the sound that goes with it. Listen to each key word as we sort it:** *catcher, picture, measure.* Point out the pronunciation key inside slash marks for each header. **Now help me sort the rest of the words, looking at the pattern and listening for the sound. There are some oddballs!**

3. After sorting, ask, **What do you notice about all the words under *catcher*?** Talk about how they all have a base word that becomes a person who does things (agents) with the addition of *er*. Probe with, **What do you notice about the base words?** They end in *ch*, so only *er* was added. **What letter is silent?** (*t*) **What can you say about the words under *picture*?** Probe with, **Do they have base words?** (No) **What sound does the *t* have in these words?** (/ch/) Repeat with *measure* and ask, **What is the sound of the *s*?** (It sounds like /zh/.) If students had trouble reading any of the words, revisit them now and apply what they have learned about final syllables spelled -*ture* or -*sure*.

4. Continue with, **What are the oddballs and why? What is the sound in the second unaccented syllable?** (/yur/) **How is it spelled?** (with -*ior* and -*ure*)

5. Ask, **What can you conclude from this sort? When do you use the -*er* spelling?** (After a base word.) **When do you use the -*ure* pattern?** (After *t* when you hear /chur/ or after *s* when you hear /zhur/.) Use suggestions under "Apply" below to develop the generalization further at another time.

6. If time allows, ask students to do the sort under your direction, and have them check for pattern and sound.

Extend: Use standard weekly routines. Students may not find a lot more words with -*sure* in a word hunt, but welcome longer words such as *exposure.* They may find more oddballs such as *manicure* or *brochure.*

Apply: Display some less familiar words for students to read: *fracture, vulture, closure.* Talk about what sound the -*ture* ending will have (/chur/). Explain, **When you hear the /chur/ sound at the end of a word it is not spelled c-h-u-r. What are two possibilities?** (*cher* or *ture*) **When is it spelled**

cher? (After a base word ending in *ch*.) **What would be your best guess for spelling these words and why: *pasture*, *texture*, and *preacher*?** Say, *Senior* has an odd spelling but there are a few more words with the *-ior* pattern. Try spelling *junior*, *savior*, and *warrior*.

Additional Words: *bleachers, preacher, marcher, fracture, juncture, venture, structure, denture, vulture, gesture, fixture, pasture, rupture, nurture, texture, lecture, puncture, closure, conjure, junior, savior, warrior, brochure.*

SORT 35   Unaccented Final Syllables (/CHUR/ and /ZHUR/)

-*cher* = /chur/	-*ture* = /chur/	-*sure* = /zhur/
catcher	picture	measure
figure	butcher	failure
moisture	rancher	capture
future	nature	treasure
teacher	mixture	senior
pleasure	creature	culture
stretcher	leisure	pitcher
injure	torture	posture

Sort 36   Unaccented Final Syllables (-EN, -ON, -AIN, -IN, -AN)

Generalization: The final unaccented sound of /ən/ can be spelled a number of ways, but the -en pattern is the most common.

-en	-ain	-on	-in	-an
broken	**mountain**	**dragon**	**cousin**	**human**
eleven	captain	cotton	cabin	slogan
hidden	bargain	carton	napkin	
heaven		ribbon	penguin	
chosen		prison	muffin	
stolen		bacon		
mitten				
rotten				

Sorting and Discussion:

1. Most of these words should be familiar, so let students do this sort independently by the headers. Bring students together to discuss the sort: **How are these words all alike?** (Two-syllable words accented on the first syllable [except *eleven*].) **What makes these words difficult to spell?** Probe with, **What is the final sound? What patterns spell the sound? What pattern is probably the most common? Can you find a word with three syllables?** (*eleven*)

2. **Let's sort again by syllable patterns VCCV, V-CV, VC-V. Which words do not fit these patterns and why?** (*Eleven* has three syllables, but *lev-en* fits VC-V; *penguin* is VCCCV because *u* is acting as a consonant; *heaven* and *cousin*.) **How can thinking of the syllable patterns help you spell these words?** (The short vowel is usually followed by double consonant letters.)

VCCV	V-CV	VC-V	oddball
hidden	broken	dragon	eleven
mitten	chosen	prison	heaven
rotten	stolen	cabin	cousin
mountain	bacon		penguin
captain	human		
muffin	slogan		
ribbon			
bargain			
cotton			
carton			
napkin			

Extend: Complete standard weekly routines. A word hunt is important to help students determine that -*en* is much more common than the other patterns, so combine their findings into a group chart. They may not even be able to find additional words with some patterns. After collecting a number of words ending in -*en* and -*on*, ask students to find all the adjectives and verbs (e.g., *broken, hidden, stolen, proven; frighten, soften, fasten, flatten*). It turns out that -*en* is generally the spelling for an adjective or verb (just as -*er* is used for comparative adjectives). Then ask students to identify parts of speech for the remaining words. Most will be nouns.

Ask students to record both the ending sort and syllable juncture sort in their word study notebooks. *Feed the Alligator* is a game at the PDToolkit that can be used to review. A simple game of *Memory* or *Match* (a variation of *Slap Jack*) works well because there are a variety of patterns to make pairs. More words could be added from the list below.

Apply: Ask students to spell several words from the list below and talk about their choices: *wooden, spoken, fountain*. What is a "best guess" strategy when spelling the final consonant? Did they think about *mountain* when asked to spell *fountain*?

Additional Words: *garden, kitten, wooden, chicken, spoken, swollen, button, apron, wagon, poison, weapon, carton, villain, chieftain, certain, curtain, fountain, basin, satin, margin, robin, pumpkin, raisin, dolphin, organ, orphan.*

SORT 36   Unaccented Final Syllables (-*EN*, -*ON*, -*AIN*, -*IN*, -*AN*)

-en	**-on**	**-ain**	**-in**	**-an**

broken	**dragon**	**mountain**
cousin	**human**	cotton
carton	captain	hidden
heaven	cabin	ribbon
bargain	chosen	napkin
eleven	muffin	slogan
stolen	bacon	mitten
prison	rotten	penguin

Sort 37   Unaccented Final Syllables (-ET, -IT, -ATE)

Generalization: The final unaccented sound of /it/ can be spelled in a number of ways, but the -et pattern is the most common.

-et	-it	-ate	oddball
jacket	edit	climate	ballet
secret	unit	private	buffet
target	credit	pirate	
racket	limit	senate	
quiet	habit		
comet	orbit		
rocket	summit		
planet	bandit		
magnet	visit		

Explore Meaning: *Racket* can mean noise or a paddle for tennis or badminton. A *buffet* can be a piece of furniture, such as a sideboard, or a meal where people serve themselves. Ask students to identify words related to space (*comet, rocket, planet, orbit*).

Sorting and Discussion:

1. Read the words and talk about any whose meanings might be unfamiliar. Ask, **How are these words alike?** Talk about the sound in the unaccented syllable, which sounds the same. Ask, **How can you sort these words?**

2. Students can sort independently, but warn them that there are some oddballs. Bring students together to discuss the sort: **What makes these words difficult to spell?** Probe with, **What is the final sound? What patterns spell the sound? What pattern is probably the most common? What are the oddballs and why?** (*Ballet* and *buffet* are spelled with -*et* but are accented on the final syllable, which sounds like long *a*.)

3. Ask, **What can we conclude about this sort?** Students will have to remember what spelling goes with each word, but a word hunt will help them discover which is more common.

Extend: Complete standard weekly routines. Create a group chart to establish which spellings turned up most in a word hunt. You may want to look up the origin of the oddballs in a dictionary with etymological information. Show students how *buffet* and *ballet* are derived from French, where the final *t* is often silent. Other words like this include *beret, fillet, sachet,* and *chalet.*

Apply: Call out several words from the list below. Ask students to spell them, and talk about their strategies: *poet, trumpet, bonnet, spirit.* Look words up in a dictionary to establish the correct spelling. Explain, **While a "best guess" strategy can get you close, check the dictionary when you need to be sure.**

Additional Words: *basket, blanket, bucket, closet, pocket, toilet, poet, thicket, trumpet, wicket, bonnet, bullet, faucet, digit, hermit, profit, exit, rabbit, spirit, merit;* oddball: *biscuit.*

SORT 37   Unaccented Final Syllables (-ET, -IT, -ATE)

-et	-it	-ate
jacket	**edit**	**climate**
secret	private	unit
ballet	target	credit
pirate	racket	limit
senate	buffet	quiet
habit	comet	rocket
summit	planet	bandit
orbit	magnet	visit

Sort 38   Final -Y, -EY, and -IE

Generalization: The sound of long *e* in the final unaccented syllable has several spellings: *y*, *ey*, and *ie*. The -*y* pattern is the most common ending, but -*ey* usually comes after *n*, *l*, or *k*. The *y* can also represent the long *i* in a final accented syllable.

-ey	-ie	-y = /ē/	-y = /ī/
money*	cookie	very*	July
monkey	movie	candy	deny
journey	brownie	dizzy	reply
valley	goalie	twenty	
turkey	eerie	cherry	
donkey	pinkie	body	
volley		story	
		berry	

Explore Meaning: Talk about the meaning of *volley* and how it relates to *volleyball*. *Deny* might be unfamiliar, but the concept of refusal should be easily understood. Ask students to complete a sentence such as *My parents are likely to deny me a(n) _____ for a pet. Eerie* (weird or strange) is also a good word to look up.

Sorting and Discussion:

1. Read the words without showing the headers, and talk about any whose meanings might be unfamiliar. Ask, **What do you notice about these words?** Talk about accented syllables and the sound in the unaccented syllable. Ask, **How can you sort these words?**
2. Students can sort independently, but bring them together to discuss the sort: **What makes these words difficult to spell?** Probe with, **What are the final sounds?** (Mostly long *e* and some long *i*.) **What patterns spell the sounds?** (-*ey*, -*ie*, -*y*) **Which words are accented on the final syllable?** (*July*, *deny*, and *reply*) **Which pattern do you think will be most common?**
3. Ask, **What can we conclude about this sort?** Students will have to remember what spelling goes with each word. However, draw attention to the words ending in -*ey* and ask, **What letters seem to come before the -*ey* ending?** (*n*, *l*, and *k*)

Extend: Assign weekly routines. A word hunt should turn up many additional words, including words ending in -*fy* (*classify* and *magnify*), where the final *y* has a long *i* sound. A combined group word hunt should establish that a single -*y* is much more common than -*ey* or -*ie* when spelling the final syllable when long *e* is heard. Check to see if any additional words turn up where the -*ey* comes after *n*, *l*, or *k*.

Ask students to write their numbers from 10 to 20 now that they have all been covered in sorts. Talk about which ones simply involve adding -*teen* to a number base word (*sixteen*) and which require a different spelling (*twelve*, *fifteen*).

Apply: Display a few, less familiar words for students to read. A word like *prairie* might look intimidating until it is broken into syllables (*prai-rie* or *prair-ie*). Display *apply* and *supply* and ask, **Does long *e* or long *i* make sense when trying to read these words?** Call a few words from the list below for students to spell, and talk about their strategies: *honey* (rhymes with *money* and has an *n*), *crazy* (long vowel is easy to spell and *y* is a best guess), *dizzy* (double the *z* after a short vowel).

Additional Words: *alley, pulley, chimney, honey, jockey, hockey, funny, happy, dizzy, jersey, genie, sweetie, zombie, bootie, rookie, prairie, duty, forty, beauty, crazy, gravy, army, fifty, empty, tidy, ruby, envy, bury, treaty, bossy, easy, lady, apply, defy, supply.*

SORT 38   Final *-Y*, *-EY*, and *-IE*

-ey	*-ie*	*-y = /ē/*	*-y = /ī/*
money	**cookie**	**very**	
July	monkey	movie	
candy	deny	journey	
brownie	dizzy	reply	
valley	goalie	twenty	
turkey	eerie	cherry	
donkey	story	body	
volley	pinkie	berry	

Sort 39   *Y* + Inflected Endings

Students were introduced to changing the *-y* before inflected endings in Sort 9, but here it is studied further in two-syllable words.

Generalization: When adding *-ed* or *-s*, the final *y* in a base word is changed to *i* after a consonant (as in *copy* to *copied*) but not after a vowel (as in *obey* to *obeyed*). There is no change before adding *-ing* to a base word ending in *y*.

	+ *ing*	+ *ed*	+ *s*
vowel + *y*	obeying	obeyed	obeys
	enjoying	enjoyed	enjoys
	decaying	decayed	decays
consonant + *y*	replying	replied	replies
	studying	studied	studies
	copying	copied	copies
	carrying	carried	carries
	hurrying	hurried	hurries

Sorting and Discussion:

1. Ask, **What do you notice about these words?** Take lots of ideas and be sure to talk about base words. Explain, **In this sort we are going to review rules about adding *-ing*, *-ed*, and *-s* to base words. Do you remember what we learned earlier about words ending in *y*?** See what students remember, but don't expect full answers yet.
2. It is probably best to do this sort together. Model, **First, I am going to look for all the words with the same base** (such as *obeying*, *obeyed*, and *obeys*) **and sort them together under the headers.** Sort the rest of the words with student help. After sorting ask, **What do you notice? Are there some base words that should go together?** Take ideas and then say, **Let's put together the words that end in a consonant + *y* and those that end in a vowel + *y*.**
3. Arrange the words as shown and ask, **What would the rules be when adding endings to a base word that ends in a *y*?** Students should see that the *y* does not change to an *i* before *-ing*. (Show them how this would look: *repliing* or *obeiing*.) The letter *y* changes to *i* before *-s* and *-ed* when the base word ends in a consonant + *y*.
4. Have students sort their own words under your supervision if time allows because the final sort is a bit different. Create additional headers if necessary with "vowel + *y*" and "consonant + *y*."

Extend: Assign standard routines. Be sure students group base words by whether they end in *-y* or a vowel + *y*. For a weekly assessment, give students several base words and ask them to add *-ing*, *-ed*, and *-s*.

Apply: To practice transfer of the rules to other words, give students these nouns from the last sort to change to plurals: *monkey, body, cherry, valley, berry, donkey,* and *turkey*. Give them these verbs and ask them to add *-ing*, *-ed*, and *-s* to change the tense: *deny, reply*. See more words below.

Additional Words: Nouns: *jockey, chimney, army, ruby, lady;* verbs: *betray, annoy, destroy, delay, survey, worry, bury, hurry, envy, deny, reply, supply*.

SORT 39   *Y + Inflected Endings*

+ ing	**+ ed**	**+ s**
obeying	enjoying	replying
hurrying	obeyed	enjoyed
obeys	hurried	decaying
hurries	decayed	enjoys
decays	carried	copying
replies	studying	carrying
carries	studies	copied
studied	copies	replied

Sort 40 Unaccented Initial Syllables (A-, *DE-*, *BE-*)

In these words, the first syllable is unaccented (*a-*, *de-*, *be-*). Some of these words appeared in a within word pattern sort (*among, awhile, because*) but are revisited here. Many rank as "spelling demons" that students struggle to spell across the grades.

Generalization: As in final unaccented syllables, sound cannot always be trusted as a guide to spell the unaccented first syllable in these words, but the words fall into categories that share similar spelling patterns.

a-	de-	be-	oddball
away*	debate	because*	divide
another*	degree	believe	direct
awhile	depend	between	upon
along*	desire	beneath	
among	develop	beyond	
against	defend	begun	
afraid			
aloud			
agreed			

Explore Meaning: *Degree* has several meanings (a unit of measurement such as 80 degrees or an academic certificate such as a college degree).

Sorting and Discussion:

1. Students can sort independently before the group discussion using the headers, but remind them to look out for oddballs. Read the words and discuss meanings.

2. Ask, **What do you notice about these words?** After sorting, read down each column and emphasize the accented syllable. Ask, **What is the sound of the *a* in the first syllable?** (/uh/ or /ə/) Review, **We call this unaccented sound the *schwa* sound. In a dictionary, it is often shown as an upside down *e* (ə). What is the sound of *de-* and *be-*?** (/duh/ and /buh/ or /də/ and /bə/) Expect some lively debate about

the exact pronunciation of some of these words. We sometimes stress a different syllable when we say a word in isolation or when we are thinking about the spelling. For example, we might say <u>believe</u> with a long *e* vowel sound at times, but when we use it in a sentence, we probably say /bə-lēv/ or /bĭ-lēv/. Stressing normally unaccented syllables is actually a good spelling strategy that works well with words like these.

3. **What are the oddballs and why?** The oddballs include a few words that have the *schwa* sound in the first syllable but a different spelling pattern.

4. **What can we conclude from this sort? What might make these words hard to spell?** (The sound of the vowel in the first syllable does not provide a reliable clue.)

Extend: Assign standard weekly routines. A word hunt is likely to turn up lots more words, but it would be even better to ask students to look through their word study notebooks for words that have appeared in earlier sorts. In many cases, these words are in sorts because of the final accented syllable, for example, *appear, before, below, defeat, delight, adore, avoid, around,* and so on. Challenge students to look for some other initial syllables that are unaccented and have the *schwa* sound, such as *to-* as in *toward* and *today,* *con-* as in *confuse* and *contain,* and *re-* as in *repeat* and *remain.* These examples will be studied later as prefixes.

Apply: Remind students that stressing normally unaccented syllables can be a good spelling strategy for the words in this sort. When reading, students might start with /ā/, /bē/, or /dē/ when they encounter an unfamiliar word, but it should be adjusted. For example, try reading *becoming, beseech, describe,* or *design* with a long *e* as a way to get close to the pronunciation, but then test it out in a sentence: *Her dress was becoming. I beseech you to help. Can you describe your dog? I'll design the poster.*

Additional Words: *again, ago, alike, alive, asleep, ahead, another, begin, beside, beware, belong, beyond, defeat, describe, despair, design.*

SORT 40   Unaccented Initial Syllables (*A-*, *DE-*, *BE-*)

a-	*de-*	*be-*
away	**debate**	**because**
degree	another	believe
divide	depend	awhile
along	between	desire
develop	among	upon
against	beneath	afraid
beyond	aloud	defend
agreed	begun	direct

UNIT REVIEW AND ASSESSMENT

Review:

If you have created group charts for word hunts, this is a good time to revisit them as a way to review which spelling patterns are most common (-*le*, -*er*, -*en*, -*et*, and -*y*). This information can be used as a "best guess" strategy, but remind students that when spelling matters, they need to check a word in a dictionary. When using a word processing program, the best guess will probably be close enough to get a list to choose from to correct a spelling error.

Assess:

See the directions for Unit Spell Check 6 on page 98 to check for retention.

Unit VII   Exploring Consonants

NOTES FOR THE TEACHER

Background and Objectives

Consonants continue to be explored at all levels of spelling. Hard and soft *g* and *c* were introduced in the within word pattern stage, but they are revisited here at the beginning and end of longer words. Whether the sound of *g* or *c* is hard or soft depends on the vowel that follows it, and this can account for some interesting spellings. The first sort in this unit looks at initial hard and soft *g* and *c*, which lays the foundation for the next two sorts, where hard and soft generalizations apply to words that end in -*ge* and -*ce*. This explains why there is a placeholder (the letter *u*) between *g* and *i* in the word *guide* and between *g* and *e* in the word *tongue*. Without the *u*, the sound of *g* would become soft (/jide/ or /tonj/).

The spelling of the /k/ sound in English is not as simple as most consonant sounds. Although students learned the final *ck* in relation to short vowels in the within word pattern stage, *ck* is revisited here in the middle of two-syllable words. Other /k/ spellings, such as *ic*, *x*, and *que*, are introduced.

Words with silent letters at the beginning (*honest*, *knuckle*) and in the middle of words (*listen*, *thought*) are also examined. *Ph* consistently spells the sound of /f/, usually in words that derive from Greek. *Gh* is often silent but can also represent the sound of /f/ at the end of words like *enough*. Students will:

- Understand that *e, i,* and *y* soften the sound of *g* and *c*
- Learn to spell the sounds of /k/ and /f/ using *ck, ic, x, qu, ph,* and *gh*
- Spell the words in these sorts correctly

Targeted Learners

These sorts are designed for students in the middle to late syllable and affixes stage. Unit Spell Check 7 on page 122 can be used as a pretest. Students who spell 90% or more of the words can move on to other features.

Teaching Tips

The standard weekly routines (pages 6–8) will work well with these sorts. The meaning of some words may not be familiar, so you should discuss these as part of the initial sort, modeling each in the context of a meaningful sentence, and revisit them later in the week in some fashion. Students should be encouraged to look up some meanings of words to add to the discussion. Reading words in phrases provides a context to deepen students' understanding of unfamiliar words. A website like Onelook provides common phrases students can read to add meaning.

A few words might also be assigned to look up for a word study notebook activity so that students become more familiar with the use of the dictionary. Students can also be asked to select or be assigned a word to explore more deeply and then share at week's end. For example, they may choose to construct a *Word or Concept Map*, or a *Synonym or Antonym Wheel* (these and other vocabulary activities are discussed in Chapter 7 of *Words Their Way: Word Study for Phonics, Vocabulary, and Spelling Instruction*).

A review activity for this unit is described at the end. Ask students to save their words each week to be used in a grand final sort.

UNIT SPELL CHECK 7 ASSESSMENT FOR CONSONANTS

Call these words aloud for students to spell on a sheet of notebook paper.

1. central	**2.** gossip	**3.** attack
4. sentence	**5.** plastic	**6.** equal
7. listen	**8.** contest	**9.** genius
10. ticket	**11.** village	**12.** guilty
13. index	**14.** answer	**15.** liquid
16. thought	**17.** trophy	**18.** address
19. vague	**20.** enough	

Interpreting Scores on Pre- and Posttests

Use the goal-setting form on page 4 to analyze and record results, and use the pacing guide on page 5 to plan which sorts to use.

- **90% or better**—Students can move on to the next unit.
- **75% to 85%**—A "gray area" where teacher judgment is needed. Examine the types of errors students make to see if there are features that can be targeted rather than doing all the sorts.
- **70% or less**—Students will benefit from doing all the sorts in the unit.

Sort 41 Initial Hard and Soft G and C

This sort shifts attention back to the initial sounds, so we recommend a teacher-directed sort. Allow extra time, or do it over two days, because it has two steps.

Generalization: *G* and *c* have hard sounds of /g/ and /k/ before *a, o,* and *u* (and also before consonants). *C* has the soft sound of /s/ before *e, i,* and *y; g* usually has the soft sound of /j/ before *e, i,* and *y,* but there are exceptions, for example, *give* and *girl.*

soft c	soft g	hard c	hard g
center	gentle	correct	gather
circle	gymnast	common	gossip
century	giraffe	contest	gallon
cyclist	genius	college	garage
cider	gender	custom	gutter
	ginger	collect	
		cavern	
		carbon	

Explore Meaning: None of these words are very obscure, but it is worth reviewing the meaning of *century* (100 years), *gender* (male or female), *ginger* (a spice), and *cavern* (cave). Talk about the meaning of *cent* (one hundredth) and how that relates to *century.*

Sorting and Discussion:

1. Prepare a set of words to use for teacher-directed modeling and display without the headers. Read the words quickly, and discuss any that might be unfamiliar. Ask, **What do you notice about this collection of words?** Take multiple points, but probe if needed with, **What do you notice about the first letters in these words?** (The first letters are *g* and *c.*) **What do you notice about the sound of those letters?** (Some are hard and some are soft.) Review the terms *soft* and *hard* by displaying the words *card, gave, city,* and *germ,* and ask, **Do you remember what you found out about *g* and *c* in words like these?** Accept students' ideas without adding to them at this point.
2. Explain, **In this sort, we are going to find out how *g* and *c* work in longer words.** Put up the headers and model sorting the key words: **I hear the soft *c* in *center*. I hear the hard *c* in**

correct. Repeat with *gentle* and *gather,* and then sort the rest of the words with student help.
3. After sorting, say, **Read these words with me and pay attention to the first sound. What are the soft sounds for *g* and *c*?** (/j/ and /s/) **The hard sounds?** (/g/ and /k/) **Does *c* have a sound of its own?** (No, sometimes it sounds like *k* and sometimes like *s.*)
4. Sort again. Push together the soft *g* and soft *c* words, and then do the same for hard *c* and *g*. Ask, **Is there another way we could sort the words with hard and soft sounds?** If needed, probe with, **Do you notice anything about the vowel after the initial letter?** Put the headers for soft *c* and soft *g* together, and put *center* and *gentle* underneath. Ask, **Do you see some other words with *e* as the first vowel?** Sort words with *i* and *y* into new columns, creating headers by underlining the vowel as shown below. Repeat with hard *g* and hard *c*. After sorting, ask, **What do you notice about the words in each column?** Talk about the word *century* and the sound of the *t* as /ch/, and how the word can be pronounced as two syllables (/sen' chrē/), but saying it actually as three syllables (/sen' chə rē/) will probably help students spell it correctly. Talk about the sound of the *t* as /ch/.

soft g and soft c			hard g and hard c		
c<u>e</u>nter	c<u>i</u>rcle	c<u>y</u>clist	g<u>a</u>ther	c<u>o</u>rrect	c<u>u</u>stom
gentle	cider	gymnast	garage	common	gutter
century	giraffe		cavern	contest	
genius	ginger		carbon	college	
gender			gallon	collect	
				gossip	

5. Have students sort under your supervision if time allows or on a second day. Ask, **What can we conclude from this sort?** Probe with, **When is *g* or *c* soft?** (after *e, i,* and *y*) **When is it hard?** (after *a, o,* and *u*) **How can this help you as a reader? As a speller?** Draw attention to final syllables by saying, **Look over these words. Are there some endings that might be tricky to spell? Why?** (There are unaccented final syllables in *center, cyclist, genius, gymnast, college, garage, common, gallon,* and *custom* where sound is not a good clue.) **Do you see some words that have both a hard and a soft *g* or *c*?** (*cyclist, circle, garage, college*) Note that the *c* sound remains hard before a consonant in *cyclist* and *circle.*

Extend: Students should repeat these sorts several times and record them in their word study notebooks. See the list of standard weekly routines for follow-up activities to the basic sorting lesson. Word hunts may not turn up many more two-syllable words with the soft *g* and *c*, but accept one-syllable words, such as *camp* and *goat*, and expect some oddballs, such as *girl* and *gift*.

To anticipate the next sort, point out the final sound and spelling in *college* and *garage*. Ask students to speculate about why there is a final *e* in those words. Remind students to pay careful attention to some of the final syllables in these words because these words can be challenging to spell, and suggest that they underline them in their word study notebooks. Ask students to save their words for a grand sort at the end of this unit.

Apply: Select some less familiar words from the list below and display them for students to decode: *canine, gurgle, gyrate, cynic, census,* or *cedar*. Review the generalization, and talk about whether the initial sound will be hard or soft before attempting to read the word. Also review open and closed syllables in VCCV and VCV words as a guide to the vowel sound.

Additional Words: *gamble, gully, gorilla, gopher, golden, gobble, genie, general, gerbil, gingerbread, gurgle, gypsy, gyrate, gently, gesture, cackle, camel, cactus, canine, candle, carbon, caution, comma, cozy, cocoa, coffee, curtain, cuddle, concern, concert, city, cedar, celery, census, central, cellar, ceiling, cereal, certain, cynic, cycle, cymbal, cyclone;* oddballs: *gimmick, giddy, giggle, given.*

SORT 41   Initial Hard and Soft *G* and *C*

soft *c*	hard *c*	soft *g*	hard *g*

center	**gentle**	**correct**
gather	circle	common
gossip	gutter	gallon
cavern	contest	college
giraffe	garage	century
custom	carbon	genius
cider	gender	collect
ginger	gymnast	cyclist

Sort 42   S and Soft C and G in the Final Syllable

Generalization: The *e* softens the *g* and *c* in other parts of the word as well as the beginning.

-ce = /s/	-cess	-ge- = /j/	-age = /ij/
notice	recess	budget	bandage
police	princess	danger	garbage
sentence	success	gadget	manage
surface	address	surgeon†	luggage
distance			package
office			village
science			message
practice			courage

†*Surgeon* may be sorted as an oddball.

Explore Meaning: Look up the meaning of *surgeon* (a doctor who performs operations). *Sentence* has two distinct meanings. A *sentence* can mean a judge's decision or a unit of language. *Recess* can mean a period of rest or an opening in a wall.

Sorting and Discussion:

1. Display the words without the headers. Read the words quickly, and discuss any that might be unfamiliar. Ask, **What do you notice about this collection of words?** Take multiple points, but probe if needed with, **What do you notice about the final syllable in these words?** (They all have *ge* or *ce*.) Review with, **What do you remember from the last sort about *g* and *c*?** Probe as needed. Hopefully they will remember that the sound can be hard or soft and *e* softens it. If students bring up accented syllables, compliment them and read through the words to find that most are accented on the first syllable but not all (*police*).

2. Ask, **How can we sort these words?** Get some ideas before explaining, **In this sort, we are going to find out how *g* and *c* work in another part of the word.** Put up the headers, and remind students that letters inside slanted lines, /j/, for example, represent a sound. Model

sorting the key words: *Notice* **ends with -*ce* and the /s/ sound.** Sort the rest of the words with student help.

3. After sorting, say, **Read these words with me, and pay attention to the sound of *c* or *g*.** Ask, **What do you notice about the words in each column? Why is the sound soft?** (It is followed by the letter *e*.) Cover the *e* in each word under -*ce* and talk about how the students would read these words if there were no final *e*: **Without the *e*, we would want to read *notice* as /notick/.** Repeat with words under -*age*: *Surgeon* might be an oddball or go under the -*ge* pattern. Talk about how *surgeon* would have to be pronounced if the *e* were dropped: /surgon/.

4. Ask, **What can we conclude from this sort?** Help students form a generalization that highlights a new role for silent *e*: It softens the *c* or *g* before it. Look for *c* and *g* in other places in the words: *science*, *luggage*, *package*. Talk about how they are soft or hard depending on what follows. **What will make some of these words hard to spell?** Suggest that students underline or highlight features that might be challenging to spell.

Extend: Assign weekly routines. During a word hunt, students may not find many more words in some categories, but encourage them to look for one-syllable words such as *race* or *huge* that end in -*ce* or -*ge*. Review the final sound in *college*, *voyage*, and *garage* from earlier sorts. Remind students to save their words for a grand sort. Review plurals by asking students to add -*s* or -*es* to these words from the sort: *princess*, *office*, *address*, *sentence*, *village*.

Apply: Select some less familiar words from the list below and display them for students to decode using the generalization from this sort: *justice*, *lettuce*, *image*, and so on. Talk about how the *e* does not mark the vowel long. Instead, it marks the *c* or *g* soft.

Additional Words: *necklace, justice, crevice, absence, announce, lettuce, fragrance, process, angel, fragile, challenge, arrange, submerge, baggage, beverage, carriage, cottage, damage, image, marriage, passage, postage, savage, storage, sausage, voyage, wreckage.*

SORT 42   *S* and Soft *C* and *G* in the Final Syllable

-ce = /s/	*-cess*	*-ge-* = /j/	*-age* = /ij/
notice	**recess**		**budget**
bandage	police		princess
surface	garbage		sentence
science	danger		manage
luggage	office		gadget
address	message		practice
package	success		village
distance	surgeon		courage

Sort 43   More Words with *G*

Generalization: Silent *u* is sometimes used to keep the *g* hard before *e* or *i*.

gu-	-gue	-g	oddball
guess	**tongue**	**ladybug**	gauge
guard	vague	zigzag	language
guitar	league	shrug	argue
guide	fatigue	iceberg	
guilty	plague	strong	
guest	intrigue	catalog	

Explore Meaning: Look up the meaning of words such as *vague* (not clear, confused), *league* (an organization), *plague* (a widespread disease but also a nuisance), and *intrigue* (plot).

Sorting and Discussion:

1. Display the words without the headers. Students may be unsure how to pronounce some of these words such as *plague* or *gauge*. Take ideas, but set them aside to revisit after the generalization has been established. Discuss unfamiliar words. Then start with, **There are some interesting things going on in these words. What do you notice?** Take multiple points, but probe if needed with, **What do you notice about the sound of *g*?** (It is hard.) **Of *u*?** (It is silent in most words.) Review with, **What do you remember from the last two sorts about *g*?** (It can be hard or soft depending on which letter follows.)

2. Ask, **How can we sort these words?** Take a variety of ideas before introducing the headers. Model sorting the key words: ***Guess* starts with *gu* and the hard sound of *g*.** Repeat for other key words and then sort the rest of the words with student help; remind them to watch for oddballs.

3. After sorting, ask, **What do you notice about the words in each column?** Talk about how the *g* is hard in all the words. Probe with, **Why is there a silent *u* in these words?** Cover the *u* in the words under *gu-* and then under *-gue* and talk about how we would read them if there were

no *u*. (The sound would be softened by the *e*.) **Without the *u*, we would want to read *guess* as /jess/ and *tongue* as /tonj/. What are the oddballs and why?** *Guard* is something of an oddball because it does not need the *u* to keep the *g* hard before the letter *a*. The other oddballs offer a chance to talk about the sound of *g* in each one. In *gauge*, there is both a hard and a soft *g*, but no apparent reason for the *u*. In *language*, the final *-age* is similar to words from the previous sort, but the *u* takes on a /w/ sound as it does in *penguin*. In *argue*, the *u* represents the long sound as well as keeping the *g* hard.

4. Ask, **What can we conclude from this sort?** Help students form a generalization that highlights how *u* isolates the *g* from the influence of *e* or *i*. At this point, revisit any words that were difficult for students to read and see if they can now read the words with the generalization in mind.

Extend: Assign weekly routines, but a word hunt will not be very productive except for words ending in *g*. Examine the words *vague*, *plague*, *fatigue*, and *intrigue*. Why not just leave off the *-ue* as in *vag* and *plag*? What is the vowel sound in each word? Why is the *e* needed? (It softens the *g* but also marks the vowel long.) Why is the *u* needed? (To keep *g* hard.) Is the *ue* needed in *league* and *tongue*?

Gu serves as the blend (/gw/) in words of Spanish origin such as *guacamole*, *iguana*, *saguaro*, *guava*, and *guano*. Students who speak Spanish might supply more words with the *gu* spelling pattern.

Apply: Briefly define the words *vogue* (in fashion) and *rogue* (troublemaker), and ask students to spell them and explain their reasons. Select some words from the list below and display them for students to decode using the generalization from this sort. Ask students to find verbs in this sort (*guess, guard, guide, shrug, argue*) and add *-ed* and *-ing* to each to review the rules for inflected endings.

Additional Words: *morgue, rogue, vogue, dialog, prologue, mustang.*

SORT 43   More Words with *G*

gu-	*-gue*	*-g*	*oddball*
guess	**tongue**		**ladybug**
gauge	zigzag		vague
league	guard		shrug
fatigue	iceberg		catalog
guitar	language		guide
guilty	plague		intrigue
argue	guest		strong

Sort 44   The Sound of *K* Spelled *CK*, *IC*, and *X*

Generalization: The /k/ sound is spelled with *-ck*, *-ic*, and *-x*. Words with more than one syllable ending in /k/ are usually spelled with *-ic*.

-ck	-ck-	-ic	-x	oddball
shock	chicken	magic	relax	stomach
quick	pocket	attic	index	
attack	nickel	traffic	reflex	
	pickle	topic	complex	
	buckle	picnic		
	ticket	panic		
		frantic		
		fabric		
		mimic		
		plastic		

Explore Meaning: *Buckle* (verb: fasten, bend, or bulge; noun: fastener on belt) and *racket* (something used in tennis, loud noise) have several meanings to look up and talk about. *Buckle* is also used in the expression *buckle down* meaning "to apply oneself." Have students look up *reflex* (acting or moving without thinking) and *complex* (difficult or complicated).

Sorting and Discussion:

1. Display the words without the headers. Read the words, and talk about any whose meaning might be unfamiliar. **What do you notice about these words?** Take multiple responses, but be sure to talk about the sound of /k/ in all the words. Then ask, **How can we sort these words?** Model sorting the key words under the headers, or let students sort independently.
2. After sorting, ask, **What do you notice about the words in each column?** Talk about the position of the patterns (*ck* comes at the end or in the middle, but *ic* and *x* come at the end). Talk about the sounds for the patterns. Ask, **What sound does** *x* **represent?** (/ks/) **What is the oddball and why?** *Stomach* ends in a sound like /ick/ but is spelled in an unusual way.

3. Ask, **What can we conclude from this sort?** Talk about the different ways to represent the sound of /k/ and where each example comes in a word. Ask, **What do you think is probably the most common pattern in one-syllable words for the final /k/ sound? In two-syllable words?**

Extend: Assign weekly routines. Compile the results of the word hunt to see which patterns are most frequent in one- and two-syllable words. Students should conclude that, while one-syllable words usually end in /k/ (*leak, work, link*) or *ck* (*sick*), words with two or more syllables usually end in *-ic*. The game *Double Crazy Eights*, described in Chapter 7 of *Words Their Way*, can be adapted to review the /k/ and *ck* spellings and also review the rules of adding inflected endings to such words.

Display these sentences to review word meanings, explore some additional features, and review adding endings: *We were relaxing at the park, picnicking by the lake, when I was attacked by ants. I panicked and jumped up and down frantically, making a terrific racket. My brother mimicked my reflexes the rest of the day.* Ask, **Is there anything unusual you notice about adding *-s*, *-ing*, or *-ed* to some of the words from our sort?** Point out *picnicking, panicked*, and *mimicked* where /k/ was added before the inflected ending. Ask, **Why is the /k/ added? What if it was not?** (*picnicing, paniced, mimiced*) **How would the** *i* **or** *e* **influence the** *c*? (The *c* would be soft.) Ask, **What do you notice about** *franticly*? **Why wasn't a /k/ added?** (The ending begins with an *l* and that will not soften the *c*.)

Apply: Select some words from the list below and display them for students to decode using the generalization from this sort. Ask students to find verbs in this sort (*attack, buckle, panic, mimic,* and *relax*) and add *-ed* and *-ing* to each to review the rules for inflected endings.

Additional Words: *track, stack, stick, paddock, ransack, gimmick, limerick, hammock, chuckle, cricket, electric, freckle, clinic, Arctic, metric, music, scenic, classic, public, skeptic, comic, annex, vortex, vertex, Xerox, perplex, phoenix.*

SORT 44   The Sound of *K* Spelled *CK*, *IC*, and *X*

-*ck*	-*ck*-	-*ic*	-*x*
shock	**chicken**		**magic**
relax	quick		pocket
attic	nickel		traffic
complex	topic		stomach
pickle	picnic		attack
panic	buckle		index
fabric	frantic		ticket
mimic	plastic		reflex

Sort 45   Spellings with *QU*

Generalization: The letters *q* and *u* together spell the /kw/ blend. *Qu* occasionally spells the sound of /k/.

qu in 1st	*qu* in 2nd	*qu* = /k/
question	equal	antique
quaint	frequent	mosque
squirrel	tranquil	unique
squirm	request	conquer
quiver	sequel	technique
quarrel	banquet	
squeaky	inquire	
	liquid	
	sequence	

Explore Meaning: A number of words in this sort warrant discussion: *quarrel* (argue), *unique* (one of a kind), *tranquil* (peaceful), *sequence* (order), *inquire* (ask). *Quiver* has two meanings (tremble; case for arrows).

Sorting and Discussion:

1. Students may be unsure how to pronounce some of these words such as *technique* or *frequent*. Take ideas, but set them aside to revisit after the generalization has been established. Discuss the meaning of unfamiliar words. Then ask, **What do you notice about these words?** Students should easily notice the *qu*. **What do you notice about the sound of *qu*?** (It sounds like /kw/ or /k/.) Ask, **How can we sort these words?** Introduce the headers and sort with student help.

2. After sorting, ask, **What do you notice about the words in each column?** Talk about the sounds of *qu* in each column. Ask, **Are there any words in this sort that look especially difficult to read or spell?** Take time to identify other features of the words in each column, such as the *ch* and *i* in *technique* that have a /k/ sound and long *e*. Notice how *tranquil*, *equal*, and *sequel* sound alike in the second syllable but have different spellings. Suggest that students underline these difficult features on their word cards.

3. Ask, **What can we conclude from this sort?** Help students form a generalization that highlights how *qu* usually has the /kw/ sound at the beginning or middle of a word but how it can also spell the /k/ sound. Review the sort from last week and the other ways /k/ can be spelled (*-ck*, *-ic*, *-x*).

Extend: Assign standard weekly routines, but do not expect students to find many more two-syllable words in a word hunt. Review word meanings on other days, and assign students to select some to illustrate or use in sentences. Call at least 10 words for a weekly spelling test. Save word cards for a final grand sort.

Apply: Display some words from the list below for students to read.

Additional Words: *quarter, quotient, quotation, quizzes, queasy, mosquito, squabble, squiggle, qualify, quantity, quality, equation, equip, acquaint, acquire, require, vanquish, sequin, plaque, opaque, critique, boutique, bouquet, clique.*

SORT 45   Spellings with *QU*

qu in 1st	*qu* in 2nd	*qu* = /k/
question	**equal**	**antique**
frequent	unique	tranquil
squirrel	liquid	quarrel
mosque	squirm	inquire
quaint	technique	sequence
sequel	quiver	conquer
squeaky	banquet	request

Sort 46   Words with Silent Consonants

Generalization: Silent letters occur at the beginning, middle, and end of words.

silent t	silent g	silent w	silent k	silent h	silent gh
castle	design	wrinkle	knuckle	honest	through
whistle	assign	wreckage	knowledge	honor	thought
moisten	resign	wrestle		rhyme	brought
listen		answer		rhythm	bought
often					though*
soften					
(wrestle)					

*High-frequency word

Explore Meaning: Talk about the meaning of *wrestle*. While it literally means to engage in a physical struggle with an opponent, it can also be used metaphorically as in "wrestling with a problem." Ask students to look up *assign* (give a task) and talk about how it is related to *assignment* (the task itself).

Sorting and Discussion:

1. Students should be able to do this sort independently using the headers, but get together to discuss. For a teacher-directed sort, begin by covering the headers, read the words together, and discuss word meanings. Then ask, **What do you notice about these words?** If someone mentions initial silent letters such as *k* and *w*, ask if there are silent letters in all the words. Ask, **How can we sort these words?** Introduce the headers and sort with student help, or let students sort independently.

2. After sorting, read down each column and ask, **What do you notice about the words in this column?** Identify the silent letters, but also talk about other features of the words, such as the unaccented initial syllables under silent *g* with the *schwa* sound (/də/ in design, /ə/ in assign,

and /rə/ in resign) or the different sounds of *ou* before the silent *gh*. The word *wrestle* has two silent letters (*w* and *t*) and can go in two categories. Ask, **Do you notice something odd about the second syllable in *rhythm*?** It is very rare for a syllable in English to have no vowel.

3. Ask, **What can we conclude from this sort?** There isn't much to say except that silent letters occur at any place in the word and need to be remembered because they cannot be heard. Ask students if they can recall other words they know that begin with *wr* (write, wrap, wrong) and *kn* (know, knee, knife, knock) or have a silent *gh* (sigh, sight, weight). Ask, **Can you find words that contain a base word that can help you remember how to spell the word?** (such as *know* or *sign*) *Soften* and *moisten* contain the base words *soft* and *moist*, and in those base words, the *t* can be heard. You may wish to point out a spelling–meaning connection that will help students remember the silent *g* in *resign* as well as learn a new word: Write the word *resignation* beneath *resign*, and tell the students, **When a person *resigns* from a position, we call that a resignation.** Ask, **What do you notice?** (We hear the *g* in *resignation*.)

Extend: Assign standard weekly routines. Students should be challenged to find more words with silent consonants, and their search may turn up many familiar one-syllable words such as *night* or *write*. Suggest that students underline or highlight difficult features in words. Call at least 10 words for a weekly spelling test.

Apply: Display some words from the list below for students to read.

Additional Words: *thistle, rustle, jostle, gristle, hustle, glisten, bristle, fasten, bustle, foreign, reign, align, resign, gnaw, gnome, phlegm, campaign, wrench, wrist, wreath, wrong, knead, knight, knock, knapsack, kneecap, hourly, exhaust, exhibit, rhinoceros, rhinestone, rhythmic, rhombus.*

SORT 46   Words with Silent Consonants

silent t	silent g	silent w	silent k	silent h	silent gh
castle		design		wrinkle	
honest		through		knuckle	
bought		whistle		honor	
moisten		resign		wrestle	
rhyme		listen		thought	
often		brought		knowledge	
wreckage		soften		rhythm	
assign		though		answer	

Sort 47   Words with *GH* and *PH*

Generalization: The letter combination *ph* represents the sound of /f/, and *gh* can be silent or represent the /f/ sound.

ph-	-ph-	gh = /f/	silent gh
phrase	alphabet	enough	daughter
physics	dolphin	cough	naughty
phantom	elephant	tough	taught
phone	nephew	rough	caught
	orphan	laughter	fought
	trophy		
	triumph		
	paragraph		

Explore Meaning: Ask students to look up *phantom* (ghost), *physics* (science of matter and energy), and *triumph* (victory).

Sorting and Discussion:

1. Read the words together, and discuss word meanings without showing the headers. Then ask, **What do you notice about these words?** Students should readily spot the *ph* and *gh*. Remind students of the words from last week that had silent *gh* (*through, thought,* etc.). More of these so-called spelling demons are revisited this week. Ask, **How can we sort these words?** Introduce the headers and sort with students' help, or assign students to sort independently.

2. After sorting, read down each and ask, **What do you notice about the words in this column?** Identify the sound spelled by *ph* and *gh* and where those letter combinations occur, but also look for other features such as the sounds of *ou*. While *ph* can come at the beginning, middle, or end of a word or syllable, *gh* appears only at the end of a word or syllable as part of the final sound (such as *laugh*, as the base word in *laughter*). Ask, **Can you find some three-syllable words in this sort?** (*alphabet, elephant,* and *paragraph*) **What syllable has the *schwa* sound that might be hard to spell?** (The second syllable in each word.)

3. Ask, **What can we conclude from this sort?** There isn't much to say except that silent letters occur at any place in the word and need to be remembered because they cannot be heard. Ask students if they can recall other words they know that begin with *wr* (*write, wrap, wrong*) and *kn* (*know, knee, knife, knock*) or have a silent *gh* (*sigh, sight, weight, bought*).

Extend: Assign standard weekly routines. Call at least 10 words for a weekly spelling test.

Apply: Display some words from the list below for students to read. It is difficult to know if *ph* or *gh* is the spelling when /f/ is heard in unfamiliar words. However, meaning-related base words and roots such as *phone* and *photo* offer clues. Students will learn more about these meaning clues as they progress to the derivational relations stage. At this point, you might ask them to spell *telephone, microphone,* and *homophone,* and talk about the reasons for their spellings. Knowing how to spell the word *phone* and understanding that the meaning of the words all have to do with "sound" will help students spell those words.

Additional Words: *sphere, sphinx, spherical, prophet, photograph, photocopy, pharmacy, pheasant, phoenix, phony, physical, phonics, phoneme, elephant, telephone, homophone, autograph;* names: *Phoebe, Sophia, Joseph.*

SORT 47   Words with *GH* and *PH*

ph-	-ph-	gh = /f/	silent gh
phrase	alphabet		enough
daughter	physics		dolphin
elephant	cough		nephew
tough	phantom		naughty
orphan	laughter		trophy
rough	triumph		taught
caught	phone		fought
paragraph			

UNIT REVIEW AND ASSESSMENT

Review:

This unit was all about consonants. For a review activity, create a grand sort of six categories using the headings below. Students can use the word cards they have saved each week, or you can make a new set of all the sorts in the unit for small groups. Label six sheets of paper, and ask students to sort their words directly into the categories and create subcategories within. Ask students to record these sorts in their word study notebooks (two per page) and to organize words under the categories. There will be some words left over, such as those that end with *-ss*, and some words may go in more than one place, such as *sequence* and *knowledge*. These later words are especially interesting and should be celebrated as ways to link the features of this unit together.

1. **Hard *g* and *c*** (Consonants *g* and *c* are hard before *a*, *o*, and *u* and at the end of words. Include words that start with *g* and *c* as well as those that end in *g* and *c* such as *music*.)

2. **Soft *g* and *c*** (Consonants *g* and *c* are soft before *e*, *i*, and *y*. Include words that start with *g* and *c* as well as words that end in *-ce*, *-ge*, and *-age*.)

3. **The sound of *k*** (There are different ways to spell the /k/ sound. Include words spelled with *ck*, *ic*, *x*, and *qu*.)

4. **Silent and consonant *u*** (The letter *u* sometimes follows *g* and *q*. Include words that begin with *gu-* and end with *-gue* as well as words spelled with *qu*.)

5. **The sound of *f*** (There are different ways to spell the /f/ sound. Include words spelled with *ph* and *gh*.)

6. **Silent consonants** (Include words spelled with *t*, *g*, *w*, *k*, *h*, and *gh*.)

Challenge students to think of other ways to sort the words in this unit. They could look for syllable patterns, vowel sounds in the accented syllable, parts of speech, or final unaccented syllables. Don't expect to include all the words in any set of categories.

Assess:

Use the unit spell check as a posttest.

Unit VIII   Affixes

NOTES FOR THE TEACHER

Background and Objectives

The term *affixes* includes prefixes (added at the beginning of words) and suffixes (added at the end of words), and both will be introduced as meaning units (or morphemes) in these sorts. Unlike the inflected suffixes studied earlier, the affixes in these sorts change the meaning of the word (*lock* becomes the opposite *unlock*) or the part of speech (the verb *love* becomes the adjective *lovely* or *loveable*). The suffix *-er*, which can indicate agents and comparatives, has already been introduced, although it was not identified as a suffix at the time. It will be revisited here along with *-est* where they are added to words that end in *-y*.

These sorts foreshadow the derivational relations stage, where meaning and the learning of new vocabulary take on greater importance in word study activities. Much more attention will be paid to the meaning of the words *after* they are sorted rather than before, so we suggest you skip the usual practice of reading and discussing the meanings of unfamiliar words as the first step. The words in these sorts (especially the base words) are likely to be words that are known to most students, and the focus is on learning about base words and affixes as meaning units that can be combined in different ways. Often the spelling of these words is not especially challenging but working with the sorts helps students think of words as being made up of "chunks" or word parts that share meanings and spelling patterns. Students will:

- Identify and spell prefixes and suffixes
- Identify the meaning of prefixes and how they change the meaning of the word
- Spell the words correctly in these sorts

Targeted Learners

We have placed these sorts here in the later part of the syllables and affixes stage as a transition into the next stage of derivational relations. However, these sorts can be used earlier if desired. Most language arts standards stipulate the study of prefixes and suffixes beginning in second grade. As long as students can read and understand the base words (such as *mature* in *premature*), they can benefit from these sorts. Words that have a familiar base word have been selected whenever possible in this introduction to prefixes. Unit spell checks can be used to determine if students are ready to study these words.

Because all these affixes (except *non-*) are covered in the derivational relations supplement, you may decide, in the interest of time, to skip these sorts entirely. Your decision may depend on the grade level and time of year. For example, many of the words selected for sorts in the derivational relations stage are challenging, not so much in terms of spelling but in terms of meaning. The words in this syllables and affixes unit will be easier and more appropriate for students in third or fourth grade than the ones in the next stage. If students reach these sorts late in the school year, it makes sense to use them as a way to introduce affixes and then use the sorts in the derivational relations supplement as a review the following year. The words are different and the order is not the same.

Teaching Tips

Some of the generalizations for these sorts are challenging. The meanings of prefixes are fairly straightforward and students can be expected to learn those, but this is not the case with the suffixes. Students should not be expected to memorize these generalizations and repeat them word for word. As always, do not state the generalization in advance of the sort. The generalizations are provided to guide the discussion in which students arrive at some helpful conclusions. The goal of these sorts is to help students see prefixes and suffixes as building blocks in longer words so that they can read them and understand their meaning.

See pages 6–8 for the standard weekly routine activities. Sorting by affixes is, in most cases, very obvious, so a blind sort with a partner is not especially effective but might be modified. For example, one partner would provide a definition using the base word, such as "build again" or "the opposite of happy," and the other partner would respond *rebuild* or *unhappy*. Ask students to look up some words in the dictionary and use words in sentences. Individual students may select or be assigned a word to explore more deeply, then share at week's end. For example, they may choose to construct a *Semantic Map*, *Concept Map*, or a *Synonym or Antonym Wheel* (these and other vocabulary activities are discussed in Chapter 7 of *Words Their Way*).

Because suffixes change the base words' part of speech [e.g., *care* (a verb) becomes *careless* or *careful* (adjectives) and *carefully* (an adverb)], this is a good time to introduce or review parts of speech as part of your general language arts program. Students will be asked to identify parts of speech as part of the group discussion and to sort by parts of speech as an extension. However, we do not recommend grading students' ability to identify parts of speech because they can be ambiguous in some cases. (Is *motor* a noun or an adjective in *motor home*?)

In several of these sorts, students are asked to recall and extend their knowledge of the rules for inflected endings, which was covered earlier. They will find that the "double, e-drop, or nothing" and the "change *y* to *i*" rules will come into play when *-y*, *-ly*, *-er*, and *-est* are added to base words.

This is a good time to introduce dictionaries that have information about the origins of words. For example, the word *rebel* does not have a familiar base word that stands alone, but it does have a root that comes from the Latin word *bellum* meaning *war*. How far you want to go with this topic is up to you and the level of understanding your students are ready to handle. Most students at this level are capable of understanding the role that Greek and Latin roots play in word meaning, but more systematic, focused, and thorough instruction will occur in the derivational relations stage. We encourage you to have at least one dictionary available with derivational information, such as *The American Heritage Dictionary*. Many online dictionaries have this information as well.

For most of the prefixes and suffixes introduced in this unit, students will find many more words in a word hunt. We suggest that you create a poster for each prefix and suffix, and continue to add words to each category throughout the unit. This will help to emphasize the power and extent of affixes in English.

Games from *Words Their Way* that can be adapted for the features explored in this unit include *Jeopardy*, *Card Categories*, *Word Study Pursuit*, *Word Study Uno*, and others described in Chapter 6. The game of *Match*, described in Chapter 5, can be adapted for affixes. *Prefix Spin* is described in Chapter 7.

Both Spanish and English have roots in Greek and Latin, and thus many prefixes occur in both languages that can be seen in cognates: *prepare/preparer*, *revise/revisar*, *intolerant/intolerante*, *dishonor/deshonra*, *misero/miserable*. The number prefixes (*uni-*, *bi-*, and *tri-*) are also used in Spanish in the same way. In other cases, the affixes may be different, and students can be asked to compare prefixes and suffixes in the languages they know; for example, the *-y* in English may be spelled *-oso* in Spanish (*windy/ventoso*).

Literature Connection

Authors and illustrators have created some colorful engaging books about words that will extend children's understanding of the features covered in this unit. Ruth Heller has a series about parts of speech, including *Many Luscious Lollipops: A Book About Adjectives* that has examples of words with suffixes and comparatives. Brian P. Cleary also has books featuring parts of speech as well as two about affixes: *Pre- and Re-, Mis- and Dis-: What Is a Prefix?* and *Ful and -Less, -Er and -Ness: What Is a Suffix?* Look for Robin Pulver's *Happy Endings: A Story About Suffixes*, Marcie Aboff's *If You Were a Prefix* and *If You Were a Suffix*, and Judi Barrett's *Things That Are Most in the World* that explores superlatives.

UNIT SPELL CHECK 8 ASSESSMENT FOR PREFIXES

A. Unit Spell Check

Call the words aloud for students to spell on a sheet of notebook paper.

1. prefix	2. bisect	3. uneven
4. prettiest	5. octagon	6. disloyal
7. carelessness	8. unicorn	9. expand
10. review	11. triangle	12. misspell
13. quickly	14. dirtier	15. incorrect
16. bravest	17. forehead	18. faithful
19. nonsense	20. noisily	

B. Unit Assessment for Meaning of Prefixes

The matching task on page 142 can be used to assess students' understanding of prefixes. Be sure to point out that some answers can be used more than once. Answer Key:

1. re- c.   **2.** dis- b.   **3.** bi- h.   **4.** mis- g.

5. pre- a.   **6.** in- e.   **7.** fore- a.   **8.** uni- d.

9. tri- f.   **10.** un- b.

Interpreting Scores on Pre- and Posttests

Use the goal-setting form on page 4 to analyze and record results, and use the pacing guide on page 5 to plan which sorts to use. See notes under "Targeted Learners" on page 139 for suggestions about placement if students score below 85% on a pretest.

- **90% or better**—Students can move on to the next unit.
- **75% to 85%**—A "gray area" where teacher judgment is needed. Examine the types of errors students make to see if there are particular features that can be targeted rather than doing all the sorts. Also consider grade level since these sorts are more appropriate for students in grades 3 and 4 than the sorts in the next stage.
- **70% or less**—Students will benefit from doing all the sorts in the unit.

Unit Spell Check 8   Assessment for Prefixes

Name _____

Match the prefix with the meaning by writing the correct letter in the middle column. Some meanings will be used more than once.

Prefix	Letter match	Meaning
1. re-		a. before
2. dis-		b. not
3. bi-		c. again
4. mis-		d. one
5. pre-		e. not or into
6. in-		f. three
7. fore-		g. badly
8. uni-		h. two
9. tri-		
10. un-		

Sort 48   Prefixes (*RE-*, *UN-*)

Generalization: Prefixes are added to the beginning of a word and change the meaning of the word. The prefix *re-* means "again" and *un-* means "not."

re-	un-	oddball
rebuild	**unable**	uncle
recopy	unkind	reptile
recycle	unfair	
refill	uneven	
reuse	unequal	
rewrite	unhappy	
retrace	unsteady	
retake	unusual	
retell	unbeaten	
review	unselfish	
remodel	uncertain	

Sorting and Discussion:

1. Prepare a set of words to use for teacher-directed modeling. Save the discussion of word meanings until after sorting. Display the words without showing the headers and ask, **What do you notice about these words?** Students might note that all the words contain smaller words. Remind them of the term *base word* that was used in the study of inflected endings. Explain, **All these words have a prefix added to the beginning of the base word, so let's sort by the prefix to see what we can find out about what it does to the meaning of the word.**

2. Put up the headers and key words, and then sort the rest of the words. During this first sort, the oddballs *uncle* and *reptile* might be included under *re-* and *un-*. They are there to help students see that these letters do not always spell a meaningful prefix added to a meaningful base word. Praise students if they notice this on the first sort!

3. After sorting, read down each column under the headers and talk about each word. **Look at rebuild. What is the base word?** (build) **When you rebuild, what do you do?** (Build something again, as in *We had to rebuild the barn after the tornado hit.*) Encourage students to generate a definition for each word using the base word when possible and supply an example. The oddball *reptile* should come up for discussion at this point and students should realize it has no recognizable base word. Ask, **What do you notice about the meaning of all the words under re-?** (They all mean to do something "again.") Repeat with the words under *un-* to establish that it means "not"

or the "opposite." **What are the oddballs and why?** *Reptile* does not suggest "again," and *uncle* does not suggest "not." These two words do not have a prefix added to a base word.

4. Help students summarize, **What did you learn about prefixes in this sort?** (They are added to base words and change the meaning of the word.) Students might be asked to write the meaning of the prefix on the headers (e.g., *re-* = again, *un-* = not).

Extend: Students should work with the words using the weekly routines, but a blind sort will not be very effective because sound is a clear clue to the category. Try a modified blind sort in which one partner defines the word ("the opposite of selfish") for the other partner to name and sort (*unselfish*). Be sure to model this to help students get started. Word hunts will turn up lots of words that begin with *re-* and *un-*, including more oddballs such as *rescue*, which look like they might have a prefix until the meaning and base word are considered. Word hunts will also reveal other subtle variations in meaning for the prefixes *re-* and *un-*, as well as words with no clear base words. Some *re-* words suggest the meaning "back" or "against," as in *restore*, *refund*, and *rebound*. For those students who may be ready to explore roots in more depth, words such as *retort*, *reimburse*, *rebate*, and *rebel* offer opportunities for checking the etymology or history in a dictionary. Bring students together to create a group chart of all the words they found with these prefixes, and continue to do this throughout the unit.

Review parts of speech and ask students to sort the words in this sort by verbs, nouns, and adjectives. All the words in the *re-* column are verbs, the *un-* words are adjectives, and the oddballs are nouns. Challenge students to use a verb from the *re-* column along with an adjective from the *un-* column to create sentences such as *They had to rebuild the unsteady bleachers before the big game* and *I am unable to rewrite the paper I lost.*

Apply: Give students the base words *cover*, *lock*, *plug*, *wrap*, and *tie*, and ask them to add *re-* and *un-* to make new words: *uncover*, *unlock*, *unplug*, *unwrap*, *untie*, *recover*, *relock*, *rewrap*, and *retie*. Ask them to define the words and use in oral sentences that show their meaning (e.g., *Uncover the cake when it is time for dessert*). Some combinations like *replug* are not officially words but they could be, and we understand what they mean.

Additional Words: *refinish, recall, recapture, recharge, reelect, refresh, relearn, refuel, unafraid, unbroken, unclean, unclear, uncover, unfriendly, unlock, unreal, unripe, unplug, untangle, untie, unwrap.*

SORT 48   Prefixes (*RE-*, *UN-*)

re-	*un-*	*oddball*
rebuild	**unable**	recopy
unbeaten	recycle	uncertain
refill	unselfish	reuse
remodel	retrace	uncle
unhappy	unkind	retake
retell	review	unusual
unfair	uneven	rewrite
reptile	unequal	unsteady

Sort 49   Prefixes (*DIS-*, *MIS-*, *PRE-*)

Generalization: The prefix *dis-* means "not" or "opposite," *mis-* means "badly," and *pre-* means "before."

dis-	mis-	pre-	oddball
disagree	**misspell**	**preschool**	precious
dislike	mistreat	prefix	
disable	mismatch	premature	
disobey	misplace	preteen	
discover	misbehave	preview	
dishonest	misjudge	preheat	
disloyal		pretest	
disappear		precaution	
discomfort			

Sorting and Discussion:

1. Begin this sort by telling students, **Spell the word *misspell*** (a word that is often misspelled). Have students speculate about why there are two *s*'s in the word, but do not offer an explanation about why at this point.
2. Read through the words without showing the headers or discussing meanings. Ask, **What do you notice about these words?** Review the term *prefixes* and probe with, **What prefixes do you see? How shall we sort these words?** Introduce the headers and key words. Students can sort as a group or independently.
3. After sorting, read down each column and ask, **How are the words alike?** (They have the same prefix.) **Let's go over the meanings of the words to figure out what the prefix means.** Go down each column and generate a definition for each word, using the base word: *Disagree* means "to not agree." *Discover* does not literally mean "to not cover," but "to make something known" or "to uncover." Find the common element in the definitions by asking, **What is the same about what these words all mean?** (They all mean "not" or "opposite of.") **So, what does the prefix do to the base word?** (It changes its meaning to "the opposite.") Repeat with each column, and help students discover that *mis-* means to do something "badly" or "wrongly," and *pre-* means "before."
4. Students probably know the meaning of the oddball *precious* and should be able to see that there is no base word whose meaning is changed by the prefix. Revisit the word *misspell*.

Ask, **What is the prefix in *misspell*?** (*mis-*) **What is the base word?** (*spell*) **So why do we need two *s*'s?** (One *s* is part of the prefix and the other *s* is part of the base word, so both must be there.) This will help them remember how to spell the word.

5. Ask, **What did you learn about prefixes in this sort? What does each prefix mean?** Students can add definitions to the headers for each category.

Extend: Students should sort their words several times and record the sort in their word study notebooks. Try a modified blind sort in which one partner defines the word ("spell wrong" or "opposite of outdoor") for the other partner to name and sort (*misspell* or *indoor*, respectively). Ask students to look up and record the definitions of two to three words in each category and use the words in sentences. Allow them to add inflected endings to make sentence writing easier. For example, using *mismatched* in a sentence is probably easier than using *mismatch*. They can also be asked to sort these words by parts of speech. The words in this sort fall into the categories of verbs, nouns, and adjectives.

Apply: Talk about how identifying prefixes can help students read and understand unfamiliar words. Display some longer words from the list below such as *misguided*, *prehistoric*, and *discontented*. Show students how to separate the affixes, and then read the base word. Ask them to hypothesize what the words mean using the base word and prefix, and then ask someone to check the dictionary for a definition.

The game *Prefix Spin*, described in *Words Their Way*, is recommended to review the prefixes in these first two sorts (*re-*, *un-*, *dis-*, *mis-*, and *pre-*). Students will be able to see how the same base words and prefixes can be used in many different combinations to form words with meanings that they can understand. The base word *cover*, for example, can be used to form *recover*, *uncover*, and *discover*. Or supply students with the prefixes (*un-*, *re-*, *mis-*, *dis-*, *pre-*) and some base words (*take*, *set*, *test*, *charge*, *able*, and *use*) and ask them to generate as many words as they can, combining the prefixes and base words.

Additional Words: *discharge, discolor, discontented, disorder, displace, distaste, distrust, misdeed, misfit, misguided, mislead, misprint, precooked, predate, prepaid, preset, prewash, prehistoric.*

SORT 49   Prefixes (*DIS-*, *MIS-*, *PRE-*)

dis-	mis-	pre-
disagree	**misspell**	**preschool**
mistreat	dislike	prefix
disable	premature	mismatch
preteen	misplace	discover
preview	dishonest	preheat
disloyal	misbehave	precious
discomfort	pretest	disobey
disappear	misjudge	precaution

Sort 50   Prefixes (*NON-, IN-, FORE-*)

Generalization: The prefix *non-* means "not," and the prefix *fore-* means "before" or "in front of." The prefix *in-* has two distinct meanings: "not," as in *incomplete*, and "in" or "into," as in *indoor*.

non-	in-	in-	fore-
nonsense	incomplete	infield	foresee
nonprofit	inactive	income	foremost
nonviolent	insane	indoor	foreshadow
nonstick	indecent	insight	foretell
nonfat	insincere		forecast
nonfiction	incorrect		forearm
nonstop			forehead

Sorting and Discussion:

1. Save the discussion of word meanings until after sorting. Display the words without showing the headers and ask, **What do you notice about these words? How could we sort them?** Put up three headers, setting aside the second header for *in-* until later, and key words, and then sort the rest of the words. Students can sort independently.

2. After sorting, read down each column and ask, **What do you notice about the meaning of the words under *non-*? Look at *nonsense*. What is the base word?** (*sense*) **What does *nonsense* mean?** (Something that does not make sense.) Ask students to generate a definition for other words in the column using the base word when possible, and supply an example such as *It is nonsense to say the world is flat*. Ask, **What is the same about the meaning of all the words in this column?** (They all mean "not" or the opposite of the base word.) Repeat with the words under *fore-* to establish that it means "before" or "in front." *Foremost* will be hard to define because it means "most important." Ask students to find four words that mean "knowing

something in advance" (*foresee, foretell, forecast,* and *foreshadow*).

3. Before going through the words under *in-*, alert students: **The prefix *in-* has two different meanings, so we will separate them as we go.** As you generate definitions, students should begin to see that some words mean "not," as in *incomplete*, but some mean "in" or "into," as in *indoor*.

4. Help students summarize, **What did you learn about prefixes in this sort? What does each prefix mean?** Students can be asked to write the meaning of the prefix on the headers. An extra header has been supplied for both meanings of *in-*. Future sorts should be under all four headers.

Extend: Sorting these words by the spelling of the prefix is easy, but try a modified blind sort in which partners define words to be sorted as described in earlier sorts. Students might select a few words from each category to look up in the dictionary and record definitions. In a word hunt, students will find many words with the prefix *in-*, but they may not have a known base word (e.g., *indicate, individual, indulge*). Collect the ones that clearly mean "no" or "in" and write them on a group chart, and continue to add to this.

Apply: Talk about how identifying prefixes can help students read and understand unfamiliar words. Display some longer words such as *nonliving, insecure,* and *forefathers*. Show students how to separate the prefix and then read the base word before generating a possible definition. Check definitions in a dictionary.

Additional Words: *nonacid, nonliving, nontoxic, nonskid, nonhuman, inhuman, indirect, insecure, indent, invisible, inhabit, invade, inmate, inland, inflate, inlaid, ingrown, forefathers, forefront, foresight, foreword, foretaste, forewarn.*

SORT 50   Prefixes (*NON-*, *IN-*, *FORE-*)

in-	*non-*	*in-*	*fore-*
foresee	**nonsense**	**incomplete**	
infield	nonprofit	incorrect	
forearm	nonfiction	foretell	
inactive	forehead	indecent	
forecast	nonstick	foreshadow	
insane	foremost	nonstop	
insight	income	nonviolent	
nonfat	insincere	indoor	

Sort 51 Prefixes (UNI-, BI-, TRI-, and Other Numbers)

These numerical prefixes come from Latin and are used in Romance languages such as Spanish, where the numbers *uno*, *tres*, *cuatro*, and *ocho* can be related to *uni-*, *tri-*, *quadr-*, and *octo-*. *Bi-* is used as a prefix in Spanish just as it is in English.

Generalization: *Uni-* means "one," *bi-* means "two," *tri-* means "three," *quad-* means "four," *pent-* means "five," and *oct-* means "eight."

uni-	bi-	tri-	other
unicycle	bicycle	tricycle	octopus
united	biweekly	trilogy	pentagon
unicorn	bisect	triangle	octagon
unique	bilingual	triple	October
union		triplet	quadrangle
unison		tripod	
uniform		trio	
universe			

Explore Meaning: Some of these words may be less familiar, so ask each student in the group to look up one word in preparation for the discussion after sorting. These words are worth looking up: *unique, unison, bisect, trilogy, tripod, trio, triple, quadrangle, pentagon.*

Sorting and Discussion:

1. Display the key words *unicycle, bicycle,* and *tricycle* and ask, **How are these words alike?** (They are things with wheels. A unicycle has only one wheel, etc.) **What do you think the prefixes might mean? What does *cycle* mean?** Demonstrate how to look up the etymology of the word to find that it comes from Greek (GK) and means "circle" or "wheel." Ask, **Can you think of other words that have *cycle* in them?** (*motorcycle* and *recycle*) **What do they mean?**

2. Ask, **What do you notice about the words in our sort?** Explain, **The "other" category is used for words that also refer to numbers but have only one or only a few examples.** Students can sort independently or sort as a group.

3. After sorting, talk about the words in each column. Unlike the words in previous sorts, these do not all have a base word, but discussion will help students understand how the prefix is related to the meaning of the words.

Start with, **We decided that *uni-* means "one," so let's think about how all these words are related. If a group of people are *united*, what does that mean?** (They form one unit.) **What do you know about a unicorn?** (It has one horn.) Supply help as needed with definitions or ask students who have looked up some words to report to the group. Under "other," start with *octopus* and *octagon* to establish that *octo-* means "eight." Explain that, in ancient Roman calendars, October was the eighth month, unlike the modern calendar, in which it is the tenth month. (*November* and *December* are derived from Latin: *nine* [*novem*] and *ten* [*decem*].)

4. Ask, **What did you learn about these prefixes?** Add labels to the headers.

Extend: A traditional word hunt is not likely to be productive, but you might suggest that students go to their dictionaries for a word hunt to see if they can find other words that begin with these number prefixes that they recognize as being related in meaning. Tell students to check the definitions to be sure. (For example, *trifle* and *trigger* do not have any connection to "three.") Also encourage students to begin checking for etymological information. The word *unicorn* is a good one to look up. The word *corn* is related to *horn* (perhaps because an ear of corn looks like a horn) and *unicorn* (derived from Latin [L]) means "one horn." Students may realize that *uni-* in *union* and *tri-* in *trio* don't really function as prefixes in these words, though they may discover that *trio* came from Italian and was formed based on an imitation of *duo*, meaning "two." *Pentagon* and *octagon* both refer to geometric shapes (*-gon* comes from Greek meaning "angles" or "corners"). Remind students of *hexagon* (six angled) and *polygon* (many angled). Draw attention to the word *bilingual*, and find out how many students are bilingual or know someone who is. Remind students of words they studied earlier, like *language* (related to *lingual* in terms of meaning), in which the *gu* had the sound of /gw/.

Apply: Ask, **If you invented a bicycle with four wheels, what might you call it?** (quadracycle) **With five wheels?** (pentacycle) **and eight wheels?** (octocycle) **If you speak two languages, you are *bilingual*. What if you spoke three languages?** (trilingual)

Additional Words: *biennial, biceps, biped, biplane, bifocals, unify, unity, universal, triceratops, trivet, trident, triad, trinity, trillion, octave, quadruple.*

SORT 51   Prefixes (*UNI-*, *BI-*, *TRI-*, and Other Numbers)

uni-	*bi-*	*tri-*	other
unicycle	**bicycle**		**tricycle**
octopus	united		biweekly
trilogy	union		unicorn
bisect	unique		triangle
pentagon	octagon		universe
quadrangle	unison		triple
uniform	triplet		October
tripod	bilingual		trio

Sort 52   Suffixes (-Y, -LY)

In this sort and the ones that follow, attention shifts to the end of the word where suffixes have been added. Suffixes are not easily defined. They do not change the meaning of a word so much as they change the way the word is used in a sentence, changing nouns to adjectives and adjectives to adverbs. What is more important is understanding that, when suffixes are added, rules apply about "e-drop, double, nothing, and change the y to i." This first sort may take two days.

Generalization: When -y and -ly are added to base words, they create adjectives and adverbs. Rules such as "double, e-drop, nothing, and change y to i" apply to the base word when adding -y and -ly.

-y	-ly	y to i + ly
foggy	**slowly**	**happily**
rainy	quickly	easily
sunny	clearly	angrily
snowy	safely	lazily
misty	quietly	noisily
stormy	loudly	
chilly	closely	
cloudy	roughly	
windy	smoothly	
breezy	(happily)†	
	(easily)	
	(angrily)	
	(lazily)	
	(noisily)	

†Words in parentheses go in the third column in the final sort.

Sorting and Discussion:

1. Prepare a set of words to use for teacher-directed modeling. Display the words without the headers, and ask, **What do you notice about these words?** There should be many things to say, but be sure to talk about how the words all have base words and -y or -ly added to the end. Explain, **We have looked at prefixes that are added to the beginning of a base word. In this sort, we will look at suffixes that are added to the end of a base word. How might we sort these words?**

2. Introduce the first two headers (-y and -ly), but set aside the third header for later. Let students sort the words independently or as a group into two categories. Talk about the key word *foggy*.

What is the base word? (fog) Explain, **The word *fog* is a noun, but when *y* is added, it becomes an adjective that means "like fog." We say "It is *foggy* outside." Are the rest of the words under -y adjectives?** (Yes, and they can all be used to describe the weather.)

3. Identify the base words in the words under -ly. **What is the base word in *slowly*?** Explain, *Slow* is an adjective, but *slowly* is an adverb that describes "how something is done" or "the manner in which something is done." Summarize by explaining, **The suffixes -y and -ly do not change the meaning of the word; they change how we use the word in a sentence. We say, *A turtle is slow* or *A turtle moves slowly* and they both mean the same thing.**

4. As a second step, review how to add inflected endings: **Remember how to add -ing and -ed to words like *stop*?** (Double the final consonant to keep the vowel short.) **Can you find some words in the sort that had to double the final letter before adding a suffix?** (*sunny, foggy*) **Do you see any where the e was dropped?** (*breezy*) **Do you remember how to make the past tense of words like *carry* and *fly*?** (Change the y to i and add -ed.) **Can you find words in the sort that also had to change the y to i? Let's put them under a different header.** Introduce the header *y to i + ly* and decide which words should be moved under that header. **Let's go through and identify the base word for each of these.** List them as they are named, if possible. **What do you notice about the base word?** (They end in y and are two syllables.)

5. **What did we find out about the suffixes -y and -ly?** This is not an easy generalization for students to understand, so offer support as needed. Do not worry if they can't repeat it all back to you. In short, suffixes do not change the meaning of the word; they change the way the word is used in a sentence or the part of speech. **What did we learn about spelling words that end in -y and -ly?** The rules are similar to those for adding -ed and -ing. Start a chart to add to after each of the next few sorts.

Extend: Assign standard routines, including a traditional blind sort where students will find that sound is a clue to the difference in spelling words with -ly and -ily. Students will find many words ending in y in a word hunt, but they will have to determine if there is a base word with -y or -ly added. (*Monkey* or *July* will not qualify for these categories.)

Apply: Give students words to practice applying the rules for adding the ending. Ask them to add -*y* or -*ly* to the following base words: *dim, nice, nip, dust, kind, busy, day, soap, bad, noise, noisy, hasty, hungry*. If students have problems with this task, review the rules more thoroughly, and include a discussion of dropping the *e* in *breezy* but not *nicely*. The *e* is dropped only before a vowel. Because the suffix -*ly* does not start with a vowel, the final consonant is not doubled in words like *dimly*.

To review parts of speech, create frame sentences such as *The weather today is* _____ and *They talked* _____. Ask students to find adjectives that describe the weather, and adverbs that can "modify" the verb *talk* (that tell how someone talked).

Review antonyms by asking students to find opposites among the words in this sort: *slowly/ quickly, quietly/loudly, smoothly/roughly.*

Additional Words: *choppy, dirty, frosty, gloomy, gritty, sandy, sweaty, thirsty, skinny, lucky, grubby, shady, badly, barely, dimly, deadly, proudly, kindly, friendly, lonely, lively, luckily, readily, steadily, sleepily, daily, gaily.*

SORT 52 Suffixes (-*Y*, -*LY*)

-*y*	-*ly*	*y* to *i* + *ly*
foggy	**slowly**	**happily**
quickly	rainy	clearly
snowy	easily	sunny
safely	misty	quietly
stormy	loudly	angrily
closely	chilly	cloudy
windy	noisily	breezy
roughly	lazily	smoothly

Sort 53   Comparatives (-*ER*, -*EST*)

Generalization: When comparing two things, -*er* is used. When comparing three or more things, -*est* is used. When a word ends in -*y*, change the *y* to *i* before adding -*er* or -*est*.

-*er*	-*est*	*y* to *i* + *er*	*y* to *i* + *est*
braver	bravest	happier	happiest
calmer	calmest	easier	easiest
closer	closest	prettier	prettiest
stronger	strongest	crazier	craziest
cooler	coolest	dirtier	dirtiest
hotter	hottest		
weaker	weakest		

Sorting and Discussion:

1. Write or share some sentences such as *I am stronger than my little brother, My Dad is the strongest in the family, July is hotter than June, August is the hottest month.* Ask, **What does the first sentence compare?** (two things) **What does the second sentence compare?** (three or more things) Explain, **Words like** *braver* **and** *bravest* **are called comparative adjectives.** (Note: Words ending in -*est* are usually called *superlatives* and you may prefer to use this term.)
2. Display the words in the sort, and ask, **What do you notice about these words?** Students should talk about how there are base words with -*er* and -*est* added to them. Review, **We call these endings** *suffixes*. Probe if necessary with, **What do you notice about the base words ending in -*ier* and -*iest*?** After the previous sort, students should recognize that these base words ended in *y* that was changed to an *i* before adding the suffix.
3. Introduce the headers, and let students sort independently. Read down each column, emphasizing the final sounds, and ask, **How are the words in each column alike?** Talk about how the *i* in words like *happier* or *happiest* has

the sound of long *e* (/hap′ ē ər/). **Do you see any base words that were changed before adding the suffix?** (The *t* was doubled in *hotter*; the *e* was dropped in *closer, closest, stronger,* and *strongest*; and the *y* was changed to *i* in all the words in the last two columns.)

4. Ask, **What have you learned from this sort? What do you need to remember about spelling these words?** Revisit the generalization from the previous sort and add to it. When a word ends in -*y*, change the *y* to *i* before adding -*er* or -*est*, but remind students that sound is a clue as well.

Extend: Assign standard routines, including a blind sort, that will reinforce the sound clue in words ending in -*ier* or -*iest*.

The book *Things That Are Most in the World* by Judi Barrett raises questions about superlatives on each page (What is the smelliest thing in the world?) and supplies an answer (a skunk convention). It may inspire your students to create pages for their own version. What is the dirtiest thing in the world? What is the lightest thing in the world?

Ask students to be on the lookout for adjectives that cannot be made into comparatives this way: for example, *good/better/best* or *bad/worse/worst*. Words with three or more syllables are usually combined with *more* or *most*: *more beautiful, most beautiful, more important, most important*.

Apply: To help students transfer their understanding of these rules to new words, ask them to add -*er* and -*est* to these words: *sad, juicy, rough, sunny, flat, lazy, safe, noisy, fine, funny,* and *lucky*. Tell students to keep in mind rules about doubling, *e*-drop, and changing *y* to *i*.

Additional Words: *sadder, saddest, smarter, smartest, juicier, juiciest, rougher, roughest, sunnier, sunniest, flatter, flattest, lazier, laziest, safer, safest, sweeter, sweetest, noisier, noisiest, finer, finest, funnier, funniest, luckier, luckiest, scarier, scariest.*

SORT 53   Comparatives (-ER, -EST)

-er	-est	-y to i + er	-y to i + est
braver		**bravest**	**happier**
happiest		calmer	easier
calmest		prettier	closer
closest		easiest	craziest
stronger		strongest	cooler
crazier		hotter	prettiest
coolest		weakest	hottest
dirtier		weaker	dirtiest

Sort 54   Suffixes (-*NESS*, -*FUL*, and -*LESS*)

Generalization: The suffix -*ness* creates nouns out of adjectives and suggests a "state of being." The suffixes -*ful* and -*less* create adjectives that mean "full of" or "having," and "without," respectively.

-ful	-less	-ness	combination of suffixes
graceful	homeless	darkness	carelessness
colorful	hopeless	goodness	thankfulness
faithful	worthless	weakness	helplessness
thoughtful	restless	illness	peacefulness
painful	penniless	kindness	
fearful	harmless	happiness	
dreadful			
plentiful			

Sorting and Discussion:

1. Display the words, and ask, **What do you notice about the words in the sort?** Students should mention the base words and suffixes.

2. Sort as a group, or ask students to sort independently. Read the words in each column. Ask, **What can you say about all these words? Name each word in the category and define it using the base word.** (*grace* + *ful* = *graceful* or "full of grace" or "having grace," *home* + *less* = *homeless* or "without a home") **Note how the suffix -*ful* is spelled with only one *l*.** The -*ness* columns are more difficult to define, so model at least three words (*darkness* is the state of being *dark*). **What part of speech are the base words? What part of speech are the words with the suffixes added?** The suffixes -*ful* and -*less* turn a noun into an adjective. Adding -*ness* turns an adjective (*dark* or *careless*) into a noun.

3. **How were some of the base words changed before adding these suffixes?** Students should see that words ending in a consonant or *e* simply add the endings that start with consonants and do not require any changes. However, base words that end in *y* must change the *y* to *i* (*happiness*, *plentiful*, and *penniless*).

4. **What did you learn from this sort?** Review the generalization with the students, but do not expect them to memorize it. Ask, **What can we add to our list of generalizations about changing the *y* to *i*?** (Change *y* to *i* before -*ness*, -*less*, or -*ful*.)

Extend: Assign standard routines. A traditional blind sort will not be very productive but students

can try defining words (for example, "full of pain, the state of being dark").

Have students cut apart the base word and suffixes, and recombine them to create even more words: *homeless / homelessness, faithful / faithfulness, hopeless / hopelessness, hopefulness,* and to create antonym pairs like *careless / careful, painful / painless, hopeful / hopeless, fearful / fearless.*

Apply: Display some unfamiliar words like *weightlessness, thoughtlessness,* or *truthfulness,* and ask, **How would you break apart these long words to read them and understand their meaning?** Work together to find the base word and break off the suffixes. Ask students to define the words and give an example (e.g, *weightlessness*—the state of being without weight, as you would be in outer space). Ask students to spell a few words such as *hopelessness* or *usefulness.* **Are the words hard to spell? Why isn't the *e* dropped from *hope* or *use*?** The suffix starts with a consonant. Without the *e*, the words would be *hoplessness* and *uslessness*!

Additional Words: *awareness, freshness, thankless, thoughtless, painless, fearless, careless, useless, grateful, boastful, truthful, hopeful, restful, helpful, harmful, usefulness, powerless, weightlessness, thoughtfulness, fearlessness, truthfulness, hopelessness, helplessness.*

UNIT REVIEW AND ASSESSMENT

Review:

To review most of the prefixes and suffixes in this unit, reproduce the handout of base words and affixes on page 158. Students should cut them apart and combine them in as many ways as possible to make words. Model how to use a base word such as *view* and the affixes to make *review, preview, viewless, viewer, reviewer,* and *previewer.* Ask students to list the words they make and to apply rules for adding suffixes such as "change the *y* to *i*." The book *Reading Rods: Prefixes and Suffixes* and related materials (available from Learning Resources, Vernon Hills, IL) also provide a concrete, hands-on review.

Assess:

Use the unit spell checks as posttests to assess mastery.

SORT 54   Suffixes (-*NESS*, -*FUL*, and -*LESS*)

-*ful*	-*less*	-*ness*	combination of suffixes
graceful	**homeless**		**darkness**
carelessness	goodness		colorful
thoughtful	faithful		hopeless
thankfulness	painful		weakness
helplessness	illness		restless
harmless	worthless		kindness
peacefulness	penniless		fearful
happiness	plentiful		dreadful

Unit 8   Review Activity

re	use	dress
un	usual	y
dis	happy	ly
mis	easy	er
pre	fear	est
in	color	less
non	harm	ful
fore	view	ness

Unit IX   Miscellaneous Sorts

NOTES FOR THE TEACHER

Background and Objectives

The optional sorts in this unit are a miscellaneous collection that explores some interesting features of words. No word study curriculum would be complete without some attention to compound words, homophones, and homographs. Compound words are revisited in Sort 55 with longer words. Homophones are first introduced in the within word pattern stage and are revisited here in Sort 56 with mostly two-syllable words. The spelling demons *they're*, *there*, and *their* are included again, even though they were first introduced in the within word pattern stage. **Homographs** (also known as homonyms) are words that are spelled alike but are pronounced differently. Easy homographs that change the sound of the vowel to change the meaning were covered in the within word pattern stage (e.g., I *read* yesterday and I will *read* today. The man with the *bow* tie took a *bow*). The two-syllable words in Sort 57 vary in meaning according to which syllable is accented (e.g., Several states pro*duce* much of the nation's *produce*). Sort 58 looks at words with the *ei* pattern to explore the generalization that the order of letters for the long *e* sound is "*i* before *e* except after *c*." This sort is included here rather than earlier with other vowel patterns because many of the words that follow the generalization, such as *deceive* and *conceit*, are probably not familiar.

During this unit students will:

- Review compound words
- Identify homophones and homographs
- Spell the words in these sorts

Targeted Learners

These optional sorts are included here at the end of the syllables and affixes stage because many of the words reflect a more sophisticated vocabulary than words in earlier sorts. However, teachers can use their own judgment about using these sorts earlier in the sequence if they feel it is appropriate. There is no spell check for this unit.

Teaching Tips

The standard weekly routines described on pages 6–8 should be used with these sorts, but blind sorts will not work easily for Sorts 55 and 56. Word hunts may not turn up many new words for some of these sorts. Sort 55 may be a good time to share etymological information about the word *compound*: It comes from a Latin word meaning "put together"; individual words are literally "put together" to form a compound word.

Homographs and homophones exist in all languages. Spelling and accents distinguish the meaning of Spanish homographs and homophones, for example, homophone pairs: *arrollo* (to roll up) and *arroyo* (stream); *grabar* (to record) and *gravar* (to worsen); and *mas* (but) and *más* (more). Some homographs that Spanish speakers will know include *listo* ("ready" or "start"), *nada* ("swim" or "nothing"), *alto* ("tall" or "stop"), and *hoja* ("leaf" or "sheet of paper").

Literature Connection

Some of the features in this unit can be explored further with children's books: *How Much Can a Bare Bear Bear?: What Are Homonyms and Homophones?* by Brian P. Cleary, *Dear Deer: A Book of Homophones* by Gene Barretta, and *If You Were a Homonym or Homophone* by Nancy Loewen. Books by Fred Gwynne are old favorites that illustrate homophones and homographs: *The King Who Rained*, *A Chocolate Moose for Dinner*, and *A Little Pigeon Toad*. Also look for Brian P. Cleary's *Thumbtacks, Earwax Lipstick, Dipstick: What Is a Compound Word?* and *If You Were a Compound Word* by Trisha Speed Shaskan. *In a Pickle: And Other Funny Idioms* by Marvin Terban deals with another feature worth exploring.

Sort 55   Advanced Compound Words

In this sort, we revisit compound words. If students set aside a section of their word study notebooks to add compound words during Unit II, or if you have been keeping a chart, this is a time to look at that collection and celebrate the large number of words in English that are compounds. See Unit II and Chapter 7 of *Words Their Way* for more ideas about compound words.

Generalization: Compound words are made up of two words joined together. Each word contributes to the meaning of the longer word.

waterfall	paperback	overnight
watermelon	newspaper	overlook
watertight	notepaper	overweight
dishwater	paperwork	sleepover
waterproof		overgrown
		pullover

underground	sunset	
underpass	sunflower	
undershirt	sunshine	
undercover	sunglasses	
	sunblock	

Explore Meaning: You might ask students to look up the meaning of a few words in advance of the sort: *waterproof, overlook, pullover,* and *undercover.*

Sorting and Discussion:

1. Show your students all the words without going over the meanings in advance (that will come later). Ask, **What do you notice about all these words?** Take various responses, but be sure to talk about how they are all made up of two words. Review the term *compound words* and define with examples: **Compound words are made of two words, such as *waterfall*, which is made up of *water* and *fall*.**
2. **How shall we sort these words?** Students should quickly spot the common elements, but

if they do not, be ready to model a category to get started. Set up the bolded key words as headers, and then sort the rest of the words with student help.

3. After sorting, read down each column. Say, **Let's talk about the meaning of each word and how the meaning relates to the two words that make it up:** *A watermelon is a kind of melon that is very watery or juicy.* Some compound words cannot be interpreted so literally. *Overlook* can name a place where you can look over the countryside, but it can also mean "fail to notice something." Students who were asked to look up the meanings of a few words can add to the group discussion.

4. Reflect by asking, **What did you learn from this sort? What is a compound word?**

Extend: Have students complete standard weekly routines described on pages 6–8. Students may enjoy selecting a word from each category to illustrate. During a word hunt, have them look for any compound word. Review any collections of compound words that students might have been keeping. Call at least 10 words aloud for students to spell for a weekly assessment.

Share books about compound words: *Thumbtacks, Earwax, Lipstick, Dipstick: What Is a Compound Word?* by Brian P. Cleary and Brian Gable, and *If You Were a Compound Word* by Trisha Speed Shaskan and Sara Gray.

Apply: Have students brainstorm other words that share these same word parts. There are many words that have *over* and *under* as part of the compound. Students might brainstorm other words or check dictionaries to find more. See the list below.

Additional Words: *bathwater, headwaters, tidewater, watercolor, waterfront, waterlogged, waterworks, paperboy, sandpaper, wallpaper, paperweight, overact, overcoat, overalls, overpass, pushover, leftovers, overhead, pullover, overpower, overcome, overhear, overthrow, overcast, undertake, underclothes, underdog, underbrush, undersized, sunrise, sunlight, sunblock, sunscreen, sunbathing, sunbeam, suntan.*

SORT 55   Advanced Compound Words

waterfall	**paperback**	**overnight**
underground	**sunset**	underpass
overlook	watermelon	newspaper
watertight	sunflower	overweight
sunshine	undershirt	dishwater
notepaper	sleepover	paperwork
waterproof	sunblock	overgrown
sunglasses	pullover	undercover

Sort 56   Homophones

You and your students may not agree that some of these homophone pairs sound exactly alike. Slight regional differences may exist for words such as *bury/berry*, *vary/very*, and *marry/merry*. Accept these as examples of how the pronunciation of our English language depends on someone's own dialect.

flour	flower	vary	very
cellar	seller	hire	higher
weather	whether	merry	marry
allowed	aloud	metal	medal
desert	dessert	chews	choose
bored	board	they're	there*
bury	berry		their*

*High-frequency word

Explore Meaning: Students can be asked to look up some words in preparation for the discussion after sorting: *bury, cellar, allowed, bored, board, vary,* and *desert* (check both dictionary entries for multiple meanings).

Reviewing phrases deepens students' access to meaning. Students can collect phrases from references like Onelook online, and then use the phrases to create sentences. For example, the words *bury* and *berry* have several dozen phrases, including *bury the treasure, bury the dead, bury the hatchet, bury your head in the sand, berry-picking, cranberry sauce, strawberry jam,* and *blackberry bush.*

Sorting and Discussion:

1. Present a pair of words like *flour* and *flower*. Ask students what they notice about them. (They sound alike but are spelled differently.) Review the meaning of *homophones* if necessary—words that sound (*phone*) alike (*homo*) but are spelled differently and have different meanings. Take the time to review collections of homophones you might have in the class or share books about homophones such as *Eight Ate: A Feast of Homonym Riddles* by Marvin Terban, *Dear Deer: A Book of Homophones* by Gene Barretta, and *How Much Can a Bare Bear Bear?* by Brian Cleary.
2. Read through the words together, and then ask, **What do you notice about these words? Let's pair up the homophones.** Talk about the meanings,

and ask students to share their dictionary findings. Be ready to supply child-friendly definitions, phrases, sentences, and illustrations. Students will typically know one homophone better than the other, but by pairing them up to compare spelling and by discussing their meaning, the new words will become familiar. They can draw simple sketches for some of the homophones. For example, a sketch of a rain cloud can remind them of the meaning of *weather*, a tombstone for *bury*, a cake for *dessert*, and so on.

3. *Desert* needs special attention because it is a homograph that means both the verb "to abandon" and the noun "dry region." The word *desert* will appear again in Sort 57, so for now settle on the verb as a homophone to *dessert*. The words *there, their,* and *they're* persist as spelling problems for many students. Review some mnemonics for remembering these words, such as *there* includes the word *here*, and *here* can usually be substituted for *there. They are* can always substitute for *they're*.
4. Ask, **What can we learn from this sort?** Explain that English has lots of homophones, and they just have to be remembered. Thinking about the *meaning* of each word in a homophone pair will help students better remember the *spelling*. Ask students for ideas about how certain spellings can be remembered: *Sellers* have *sales*, while *cellars* might have jail *cells*; there are two *s*'s in *dessert* because you always want more.

Extend: Ask students to record pairs in their word study notebooks and use some in sentences. Partners might work together to make up sentences that contain both the words, such as *I was not sure* <u>whether</u> *the* <u>weather</u> *would be good enough to plan a party outdoors.* The students can share these sentences with each other. Other routines such as a blind sort or a word hunt are not recommended. Instead, partners can turn their words over and play *Memory* or *Concentration* to find homophone pairs. *Homophone Solitaire* is described in Chapter 7 of *Words Their Way. Homophone Rummy* and *Win, Lose, or Draw*, described in Chapter 6 of *Words Their Way*, will also review and extend the study of homophones.

Additional Words: *fairy/ferry, capitol/capital, morning/mourning, ceiling/sealing, cereal/serial, naval/navel, pedal/peddle, patients/patience, profit/prophet, symbol/cymbal, lessen/lesson, principal/principle.*

SORT 56   Homophones

flower	flour	cellar
very	seller	bury
weather	bored	vary
hire	desert	board
berry	whether	metal
chews	higher	aloud
allowed	dessert	medal
merry	choose	marry
they're	there	their

Sort 57   Homographs

In the within word pattern stage, students studied homographs such as *lead*, *read*, and *live*, which vary by vowel sound. The words in this sort vary by accented syllable.

Generalization: Homographs are spelled the same but have different pronunciations and meanings.

noun	verb
present	pre**sent**
desert	de**sert**
record	re**cord**
permit	per**mit**
rebel	re**bel**
object	ob**ject**
subject	sub**ject**
reject	re**ject**
produce	pro**duce**
conduct	con**duct**
export	ex**port**
contract	con**tract**

Explore Meaning: Many of these words may be unfamiliar to students, but looking up words in advance of the discussion might prove confusing when there are two pronunciations and multiple meanings. Provide support during the sort, and continue to review meanings through the weekly activities. In your pronunciation of the words, emphasize the accented syllables to show meaning changes (**reb**el/re**bel**).

Sorting and Discussion:

1. These words are best presented in context, so look for sample sentences on page 166 and display them in some fashion. Begin with the sentence: *It was time to present the present.* Ask, **What do you notice about the words** pre *sent* **and** *pres* ent**?** Students should note that the words are spelled the same but sound slightly different. Explain, **These words are called** *homographs*, **which means "same writing" or "same letters."** You might point out how this term is related to *homophone*, which means "same sound."

2. Display the words, but set aside the headers for now. Explain, **In these words, the accented syllable is in bold type, so let's sort them first by accent before we try reading them.** Sort

quickly by the accented syllable, matching pairs as you go. After sorting, read down each column stressing the accented syllable. Ask, **What do you notice about the words in each column?** Students might note that many of the words have prefixes.

3. Go back to the sentence featuring *present* and ask, **Which word is a thing or a noun?** (**pres**ent) **Which one is something you do or is a verb?** (pre**sent**) Use the other sentences to introduce the rest of the words. For each one ask, **What do the words mean? Which is a noun? Which is a verb?** Place the words under the headers *noun* or *verb*.

4. When all the words have been sorted, read down each column again, placing extra emphasis on the accented syllable. Ask, **What do you notice about the words in each column?** (The nouns are accented on the first syllable and the verbs are accented on the second syllable.) Say, **Let's try reading each pair of words by changing the accent.** Expect this exercise to be difficult without context.

5. **What can we learn from this sort as readers and spellers?** In English, some words spelled the same way can be pronounced in different ways, and the context of the sentence may be needed to know how to pronounce the words. For many words, the noun form is accented on the first syllable, while the verb form is accented on the second syllable.

Extend: Students can complete weekly routines, but do not expect them to find more homographs in a word hunt. Partners in a blind sort will have to pronounce the words carefully and perhaps use them in a sentence before asking their buddy to sort them by accent or part of speech. Skip this if you think it is too difficult for students. Ask students to select up to 10 unfamiliar words to look up in the dictionary. Ask them to indicate the correct accented syllable to go with the definition.

Apply: Pair students to read the sentences on page 167. Talk about how they may need to try a word several ways to get the right stress. Challenge them to mark the accented syllables in the homographs by underlining or using an accent mark. Select words from the list below to create your own sentences for students to read or challenge students to write their own.

Additional Words: *address, minute* (noun and adjective), *project, refuse, insert, insult, survey, wound.*

SORT 57   Homographs

noun	verb	
present	present	desert
record	permit	rebel
permit	desert	record
rebel	subject	object
reject	object	subject
produce	conduct	export
conduct	reject	produce
contract	export	contract

Homograph Sentences for Use with Sort 57:

1. It was time to pre<u>sent</u> the pre<u>sent</u>.
2. It was a mistake for the soldier to de<u>sert</u> in the <u>des</u>ert.
3. The athlete hoped to re<u>cord</u> a new world <u>rec</u>ord.
4. They would not per<u>mit</u> us to have the parade without a <u>per</u>mit.
5. The <u>reb</u>el was trying to re<u>bel</u> against the king.
6. Mom will ob<u>ject</u> to that ugly <u>ob</u>ject on the coffee table.
7. I had to sub<u>ject</u> the <u>sub</u>ject to a series of tests.
8. If they re<u>ject</u> my application, I will feel like a <u>re</u>ject.
9. The farm was used to pro<u>duce</u> fresh <u>pro</u>duce for local restaurants.
10. They will con<u>duct</u> an investigation of the player's <u>con</u>duct.
11. Bananas are an <u>ex</u>port from countries that ex<u>port</u> fruit.
12. My builder cannot sign the <u>con</u>tract until I con<u>tract</u> a plumber.

Homograph Sentences for Use with Sort 57

Name _____

Read the homographs in the sentences below. Underline the syllable in each homograph that should be accented to make the meaning clear.

1. It was time to present the present.

2. It was a mistake for the soldier to desert in the desert.

3. The athlete hoped to record a new world record.

4. They would not permit us to have the parade without a permit.

5. The rebel was trying to rebel against the king.

6. Mom will object to that ugly object on the coffee table.

7. I had to subject the subject to a series of tests.

8. If they reject my application, I will feel like a reject.

9. The farm was used to produce fresh produce for local restaurants.

10. They will conduct an investigation of the player's conduct.

11. Bananas are an export from countries that export fruit.

12. My builder cannot sign the contract until I contract a plumber.

Sort 58   *I* Before *E* Except After *C*

Many adults still rely on the "*i* before *e* except after *c*" spelling rule, so this is worth teaching, even though it applies to a fairly small number of words.

Generalization: The sound of long *e* is sometimes spelled *ie* or *ei*. After *c*, the pattern is always *ei*. However, the *ei* pattern can also spell the long *a* sound. The complete old jingle goes like this: "*i* before *e* except after *c* or when sounded like *a* as in *neighbor* and *weigh*."

ie = long e	ei = long e	cei = long e	ei = long a	oddball
thief	seize	receive	neighbor	mischief
niece	weird	ceiling	eighteen	
priest	either	deceive	weigh	
grief	neither	conceit	sleigh	
shield		receipt	freight	
relieve			reign	
yield				
belief				

Explore Meaning: Ask students to look up some of these words: *relieve* (help or lessen, as in *relieve pain*), *receive* (take in), *deceive* (mislead or trick), *conceit* (self-importance), *receipt* (proof of purchase), and *freight* (goods transported by land, sea, or air). See if students can add additional words to match, like *relief/relieve*, *deceit/deceive*, *conceive/conceit*, *belief/believe*.

Sorting and Discussion:

1. This is best done as a teacher-directed sort because it involves several steps. Set aside the headers for now. Begin by going over the words to pronounce, and talk about the meaning of any words students might not know. Ask, **What do you notice about these words?** The letters *e* and *i* are somewhat complicated in these words! **How can we sort these words?** There are several possibilities, but suggest starting with a sound sort.

2. Put up the key words *thief* and *neighbor* as headers for a sound sort. Ask students to listen for the vowel sound in each word: **Thief has the long *e* sound, and *neighbor* has the long *a* sound. Let's find other words with those sounds.** Sort the rest of the words with the students' help by the sound of the vowel in the accented syllable. The word *mischief* will be an oddball.

3. Ask, **What spelling patterns do you see under long *e*?** Use *thief* and *seize* as key words and sort the rest of the words under them by pattern. Ask, **What makes these words hard to spell?** (Not knowing whether to use *ie* or *ei* because the sound is the same.) Explain, **There is one thing that will help. Can you find words in which the *ei* comes after the letter *c*?** Put these words in another column and ask, **How are the words in each column alike?** Put up the headers as you review each column. **What is the oddball and why?** (*Mischief* has the short *i* sound spelled with *ie*.)

4. Talk about some of the other features of these words. **Why is the *c* soft in many of these words?** (It is followed by *e* or *i*.) Ask, **What are some other things besides the vowel patterns that make these words hard to spell?** Prompt with, **Why does *niece* end in *e*?** (To soften the *c*.) **What other words end in silent *e* but do not need a vowel marker?** (*relieve, seize, receive,* and *deceive*) **Note:** Students studied this silent *e* feature in the within word pattern stage in words like *freeze* and *leave*. Ask, **Can you find some words with silent consonants?** (All the words under long *a* have a silent *g* or *gh*, and there is a silent *p* in *receipt*.) Suggest that students underline or highlight these features to help them remember them.

5. Ask, **What can we conclude from this sort?** These words can be hard to spell. Share the saying: *i* before *e* except after *c* and when sounded as *a* as in *neighbor* and *weigh*. Talk about how well this rule covers the words in the sort. (It does not account for the words under *seize*.) Explain that the rule does help spellers to remember how to spell the words that have *cei*, but we just have to memorize how to spell the others.

Extend: Standard weekly routines that include blind sorts will give students practice in mastering these words. Word hunts will not turn up much because only a small number of words are spelled with *ei* and *ie*.

Apply: Explain that words like these are spelling challenges even for adults. **What would help you spell a word like *perceive*?** (Thinking of a rhyming word like *deceive* or *receive* and remembering that after *c* the pattern is *ei*.)

Additional Words: *protein, deceit, perceive, conceive, eight, eighty, leisure.*

SORT 58   *I* Before *E* Except After *C*

ie = /ē/	*cei* = /ē/	*ei* = /ē/	*ei* = /ā/
thief	**receive**		**neighbor**
seize	niece		ceiling
eighteen	weigh		priest
deceive	weird		sleigh
grief	shield		either
receipt	mischief		relieve
yield	belief		freight
neither	reign		conceit

Appendix

Blank Template for Word Sorts

Appendix

Word Study Homework Form

Name _____ Date _____

Cut apart your words and sort them first. Then write your words below under a key word.

_____

_____

_____

_____

_____

_____

_____

_____

_____

_____

What did you learn about words from this sort?

_____

_____

_____

On the back of this paper write the same key words you used above. Ask someone to shuffle your word cards and call them aloud as you write them into categories. Look at each word as soon as you write it. Correct it if needed.

Check off what you did and ask a parent to sign below.
_____ Sort the words again in the same categories you did in school.
_____ Write the words in categories as you copy the words.
_____ Do a blind sort with someone at home.
_____ Write the words into categories as someone calls them aloud.
_____ Find more words in your reading that have the same sound and/or pattern. Add them to the categories on the back.
Signature of Parent _____

Word Sort Corpus
Numbers refers to the sort in which the word appears.

able	31	appoint	24	barely	26	bottle	31
about*	24	approach	20	bargain	36	bottom	14
acted	5	April	32	basic	18	bought	46
actor	34	argue	43	battle	31	bowling	20
address	42	around*	24	beauty	21	bracelet	18
adhere	30	ashes	7	because*	40	branches	7
adore	27	ashore	27	before*	27	brave	1
advice	19	assign	46	beggar	34	braver	53
afraid	40	athlete	16	begging	4	bravest	53
after*	14	attack	44	begun	40	breezy	52
again*	18	attic	44	belief	58	brief	1
against	40	auction	25	believe	40	brighter	34
agreed	40	August	25	below	20	brightly	19
airplane	26	author	25	benches	7	broken	36
allow	25	autumn	25	beneath	40	brother	33
allowed	56	avoid	24	berry	38, 56	brought	46
alone	20	awake	18	beside	12	brownie	38
along*	40	aware	26	better*	14	brushes	7
aloud	40, 56	away*	40	between	40	buckle	44
alphabet	47	awesome	25	beware	26	budget	42
also*	25	awful	25	beyond	40	buffet	37
alter	25	awhile	40	bicycle	51	bugle	31
although	25	awkward	25	bigger	34	burger	29
always*	25	awoke	20	bilingual	51	burglar	34
amaze	18	baby	18	birdbath	29	bury	56
among	40	backbone	11	birthday	29	busy	13
amount	24	backfire	11	bisect	51	butcher	35
amuse	21	background	11	biweekly	51	cabin	36
angel	32	backpack	11	blanket	14	cable	31
angle	32	backtrack	11	bled	6	calmer	53
angrily	52	backward	28	bleed	6	calmest	53
annoy	24	backyard	11	board	56	candle	31
another*	40	bacon	36	body	38	candy	38
answer	46	ballet	37	bony	23	captain	36
antique	45	balloon	21	bookcase	10	capture	35
anyone	12	bandage	42	bookmark	10	carbon	41
anything*	12	bandit	37	books	7	careful	26
appear	30	banquet	45	border	27	carelessness	54
apple	31	barber	26	bored	56	carpet	26

*A word that occurs in the top 300 high-frequency words

carried	39	cleaning	3	copying	39	deceive	58
carries	39	clearly	52	corner	27	decide	19
carrot	26	climate	37	correct	41	decode	20
carry*	26	climb	1	cotton	36	deer	8
carrying	39	clog	1	cough	47	defeat	22
carton	36	closed	5	countdown	10	defend	40
cartoon	21	closely	23, 52	counter	24	degree	40
castle	46	closer	53	country	24	delay	23
catalog	43	closest	53	county	24	delight	19
catcher	35	closing	3	courage	42	deny	38
cattle	32	clothes	7	cousin	36	depend	40
caught	47	cloudy	52	coward	24	describe	19
caution	25	coaster	20	cradle	31	desert	56, 57
cavern	41	cocoon	21	crashes	7	design	46
ceiling	58	collar	33	crayon	18	desire	40
cellar	56	collect	41	crazier	53	dessert	56
center	41	college	41	craziest	53	destroy	24
century	41	color*	33	crazy	13	develop	40
chairs	7	colorful	54	create	16	diet	16
changes	7	combine	19	creature	35	diner	13
chapter	14	comet	37	credit	37	dinner	13
chatted	17	coming	4	cried	9	direct	40
checkout	12	common	41	cries	9	dirtier	53
cheerful	30	compete	22	crisis	19	dirtiest	53
cheering	4	complain	18	cruel	16	dirty	29
cherry	38	complete	16	cry	9	disable	49
chewed	5	complex	44	crying	9	disagree	49
chews	56	compose	20	culture	35	disappear	49
chewy	21	conceit	58	custom	41	discomfort	49
chicken	44	conduct	57	cutting	4	discover	49
chief	1	confuse	21	cyclist	41	dishonest	49
children	16	conquer	45	dairy	26	dishwater	55
chilly	52	contain	23	dancer	34	dislike	49
choose	56	contest	41	danger	42	disloyal	49
chorus	27	contract	57	darkness	54	disobey	49
chosen	36	control	16	daughter	47	distance	42
churches	7	cookbook	10	daylight	10	ditches	7
cider	41	cookie	38	debate	23, 40	divide	19, 40
circle	41	cooler	53	decay	18	dizzy	38
circus	29	coolest	53	decayed	39	doctor	33
city	19	copied	39	decaying	39	dollar	33
classes	7	copies	39	decays	39	dolphin	47

*A word that occurs in the top 300 high-frequency words

donkey	38	eerie	38	female	14	Friday	19
doodle	21	eighteen	58	fever	22	fried	9
doorway	11	either	58	fewer	21	fries	9
double	24	elephant	47	fifteen	22	frighten	19
downhill	10	eleven	36	figure	35	front	1
downpour	10	employ	24	final	32	froze	6
downstairs	10	endure	30	finger	14	frozen	20
downtown	10	English	16	finish	15	fruit	1
dragon	36	enjoyed	39	firmly	29	fry	9
draw	6	enjoying	39	fixing	4	frying	9
dreadful	54	enjoys	39	flashlight	10	funny*	14
dreamer	34	enough	47	flavor	18	furnish	29
dreaming	3	equal	45	flawless	25	further	29
dreary	30	erode	20	floated	17	future	35
drew	6	error	33	floating	4	gadget	42
drive	6	escape	18	florist	27	gallon	41
driver	34	Europe	20	flour	56	garage	41
driveway	11	even	22	flower	33, 56	garbage	42
dropped	5	every*	29	foggy	52	garden	26
drove	6	everyone	12	follow	14	gather	41
drowsy	24	everything	12	foolish	23	gauge	43
duet	16	evil	32	foot	8	gawking	25
during	29	explain	18	forearm	50	geese	8
dusted	17	explode	20	forecast	50	gender	41
duty	14	explore	27	forehead	50	genius	41
dwarf	28	export	57	foremost	50	gentle	41
eager	15	expose	23	foresee	50	getting	2
eagle	23	extreme	22	foreshadow	50	giant	16
earache	11	fable	18	forest	27	giggle	31
eardrum	11	fabric	44	foretell	50	ginger	41
early*	30	failure	35	forty	27	giraffe	41
earnest	30	fairy	26	fossil	32	goalie	38
earplug	11	faithful	54	fought	47	going	4
earring	11	farmer	34	fourteen	27	goodness	54
earthquake	30	faster	34	foxes	7	goose	8
easier	53	father	33	frantic	44	gossip	41
easiest	53	fatigue	43	freedom	22	grabbed	5
easily	52	faucet	25	freeze	6	graceful	54
eastern	22	favor	33	freezer	23	grammar	33
easy	15	fearful	54	freight	58	grateful	18
eating	3	feather	22	frequent	45	greeted	17
edit	37	feet	8	fresher	34	grief	58

*A word that occurs in the top 300 high-frequency words

grinning	4	hidden	36	indoor	50	laughed	25
groan	1	higher	56	infield	50	laughter	47
growling	4	highway	19	inform	27	laundry	25
guard	43	hiking	4	injure	35	lawyer	25
guess	43	himself	12	inquire	45	lazily	52
guesses	7	hire	56	insane	50	lazy	15
guest	43	homeless	54	inside	12	leader	15
guide	43	homemade	11	insight	50	leaf	8
guilty	43	homesick	11	insincere	50	league	43
guitar	43	homestretch	11	inspect	16	leaking	17
gutter	41	hometown	11	insure	30	learner	30
gymnast	41	homework	11	intrigue	43	leashes	7
habit	37	honest	46	invade	23	leather	22
haircut	26	honor	46	invite	19	leaves	8
halfway	16	hoped	5	itself	12	leisure	35
hallway	11	hopeless	54	jacket	37	lemon	15
handle	31	hoping	17	jewel	21	lesson	13
happen	14	hopped	5	jogger	34	letter	13
happier	53	hopping	17	jogging	4	level	32
happiest	53	horrid	27	joined	5	life	8
happily	52	hotter	53	joking	17	lifeboat	11
happiness	54	hottest	53	journal	32	lifeguard	11
happy*	13	human	15, 36	journey	38	lifelike	11
harbor	33	humming	4	July	38	lifelong	11
hardly	26	humor	15	jumping	2	lighter	23
harmless	54	hundred	16	jungle	31	lighthouse	10
harvest	26	hunted	17	keep	6	lightning	19
haunted	25	hurried	39	kept	6	lightweight	10
having	4	hurries	39	kindness	54	limit	15, 37
headache	10	hurry	29	kingdom	16	lion	16
headfirst	10	hurrying	39	kisses	7	liquid	45
headlight	10	iceberg	43	kitchen	16	listen	46
headphones	10	idol	19	kitten	13	little*	31
headstrong	10	ignore	27	knew	6	lived	5
healthy	22	illness	54	knife	8	lives	8
heaven	36	inactive	50	knives	8	living	4
heavy	22	include	21	know	6	loaf	8
hello	13	income	50	knowledge	46	loafer	20
helped	5	incomplete	50	knuckle	46	loaves	8
helplessness	54	incorrect	50	ladybug	43	local	32
hermit	29	indecent	50	language	43	lonely	20
herself	12	index	44	later	13	lonesome	20

*A word that occurs in the top 300 high-frequency words

longer	34	misty	52	niece	58	overnight	55
looking	3	mitten	36	ninety	19	overweight	55
loudly	52	mixed	5	nodded	5	owner	20
lower	20	mixes	7	noisily	52	package	42
loyal	24	mixture	35	noisy	24	painful	54
luggage	42	moaning	3	nonfat	50	painter	18
lunches	7	model	32	nonfiction	50	panic	44
machine	19	moisten	46	nonprofit	50	panting	17
magic	44	moisture	35	nonsense	50	paper	13
magnet	37	moment	14	nonstick	50	paperback	55
mailing	3	money*	38	nonstop	50	paperwork	55
manage	42	monkey	38	nonviolent	50	parade	18
maple	31	monster	16	noodle	21	paragraph	47
marble	32	moody	23	northern	27	pardon	26
market	26	morning*	27	notebook	10	parents	26
marry	26, 56	mosque	45	notepaper	55	partner	26
mature	30	mother*	33	nothing	12	passed	5
maybe	18	motor	33	notice	42	passing	2
meaning	22	mountain	36	novel	32	pasted	17
measure	35	mouse	8	number*	14	pattern	14
medal	56	movie	38	obey	18	payment	18
meeting	15	moving	4	obeyed	39	peacefulness	54
member	14	muffin	36	obeying	39	peaches	7
mermaid	29	mushroom	16	obeys	39	peanut	15
merry	56	music	15, 21	object	57	pebble	32
message	42	myself*	12	octagon	51	pencil	32
metal	32, 56	named	5	October	51	penguin	36
meter	23	napkin	36	octopus	51	penniless	54
mice	8	narrow	26	office	42	penny	13
middle	31	nature	35	often	46	pentagon	51
mimic	44	naughty	47	older	34	people	22
minus	19	nearby	30	only*	14	perfect	29
minute	15	nearly	30	open*	13	perform	27
mirror	33	needed	17	orbit	27, 37	permit	57
misbehave	49	needle	22	order*	27	person	29
mischief	58	neighbor	58	orphan	47	phantom	47
misjudge	49	neither	58	other*	33	phone	1, 17
mismatch	49	nephew	47	outside	12	phrase	47
misplace	49	nervous	29	oval	32	physics	47
misspell	49	never*	14	over*	13	picking	2
mistake	18	newspaper	55	overgrown	55	pickle	44
mistreat	49	nickel	32, 44	overlook	55	picnic	44

*A word that occurs in the top 300 high-frequency words

picture	35	prettiest	53	recess	42	rotten	36
pilgrim	16	pretty*	13	recopy	48	rough	47
pillow	14	preview	49	record	27, 57	roughly	52
pilot	15	priest	58	recycle	48	ruby	23
pinkie	38	princess	42	reduce	21	ruler	21
pirate	37	prison	36	refill	48	rumor	33
pitcher	35	private	37	reflex	44	running	2
places	7	problem	14	rehearse	30	safely	52
plague	43	produce	57	reign	58	safety	23
planet	15, 37	provide	23	reject	57	said	6
planned	5	puddle	31	relax	44	sailor	34
plastic	44	pullover	55	relieve	58	salty	25
play	9	pumpkin	16	remain	18	salute	23
played	9	puppy	13	remodel	48	sample	31
playing	9	purple	29	remote	20	saucer	25
plays	9	pushing	4	repeat	22	sausage	25
pleasant	22	quadrangle	51	replied	39	saved	5
pleasure	35	quaint	45	replies	39	say	6
plentiful	54	quarrel	28, 45	reply	38	scale	1
plot	1	quarter	28	replying	39	science	42
plotting	17	question	45	report	27	scooter	21
pocket	44	quick	44	reptile	48	scored	5
poem	16	quickly	52	request	45	scout	1
poet	16	quiet	37	resign	46	scrapbook	10
poison	24	quietly	52	resting	2	season	22
police	42	quit	1	restless	54	second	15
polite	19	quiver	45	retake	48	secret	37
pony	20	quote	1	retell	48	secure	30
posture	35	quoted	17	retrace	48	seemed	5
powder	24	rabbit	13	reuse	48	seize	58
practice	42	raccoon	21	review	48	seller	56
precaution	49	racing	17	rewrite	48	senate	37
precious	49	racket	37	rhyme	46	senior	35
prefix	49	rainy	52	rhythm	46	sentence	42
preheat	49	raisin	18	ribbon	36	sequel	45
premature	49	rancher	35	rifle	31	sequence	45
prepare	26	reading	4	riot	16	serpent	29
preschool	49	reason	15	rival	19	setting	4
present	15, 57	rebel	57	river	15	settle	31
preteen	49	rebuild	48	robot	20	seven*	15
pretest	49	receipt	58	rocket	37	severe	30
prettier	53	receive	58	rooster	21	shampoo	21

*A word that occurs in the top 300 high-frequency words

sharing	4	snowing	4	started	5	survive	19
sharp	1	snowman	10	stay	9	swallow	28
sheep	8	snowplow	10	stayed	9	swarm	28
shield	58	snowstorm	10	staying	9	sweater	22
shine	6	snowy	52	stays	9	sweep	6
shock	44	soapy	20	steady	22	swept	6
shone	6	soda	23	stepped	5	swimmer	34
shopper	34	sofa	20	stirred	5	swimming	2
shorter	27	soften	46	stolen	36	table	31
shouted	5	solar	33	stomach	44	talking	4
shouting	17	somebody	12	stopping	4	tardy	26
shower	24	somehow	12	stormy	27, 52	target	37
shrug	43	someone	12	story	38	taught	47
shutting	2	something	12	stretcher	35	taxes	7
sideways	12	sometime	12	strong	43	teacher	35
signal	32	somewhere	12	stronger	53	teardrop	30
silent	14	sorry	27	strongest	53	technique	45
silver	33	speaker	23	student	15, 21	teeth	8
simple	31	spearmint	30	studied	39	telling	17
sincere	30	special	32	studies	39	thank	1
single	31	speeches	7	studying	39	thankfulness	54
sister*	14, 33	spelling	4	sturdy	29	their*	56
sitting	2	spider	33	subject	57	theme	1
skated	17	spied	9	succeed	22	themselves	12
skating	3	spies	9	success	42	there*	56
skipped	17	spirit	29	sugar	33	they're	56
skipping	2	splashes	7	summer	13	thief	58
sleep	6	spray	9	summit	37	thirsty	29
sleepover	55	sprayed	9	sunblock	55	thirteen	22
sleigh	58	spraying	9	sunflower	55	thirty	29
slept	6	sprays	9	sunglasses	55	though*	46
slid	6	spy	9	sunlight	10	thought	46
slide	6	spying	9	sunny	52	thoughtful	54
slightly	19	squad	28	sunset	55	thousand	24
slogan	36	squash	28	sunshine	55	threw	6
slowly	23, 52	squeaky	45	super	13	through	46
smaller	34	squirm	45	supper	13	throughout	12
smell	1	squirrel	45	suppose	20	throw	6
smoother	34	stain	1	supreme	22	Thursday	29
smoothly	52	stairway	11	surface	42	ticket	44
sneaker	15	stampede	23	surgeon	42	tickle	31
snowflake	10	standing	2	surprise	19	tiger	13

*A word that occurs in the top 300 high-frequency words

tiny	13	tutor	34	visit	15, 37	whistle	46
title	31	twenty	38	visor	23	wife	8
toaster	20	twig	1	volley	38	window	14
today*	18	unable	48	voter	34	windy	52
tongue	43	unbeaten	48	vowel	32	winning	17
tonight	19	uncertain	48	voyage	24	winter	14
tooth	8	uncle	48	wagon	15	without	12
toothache	21	under*	33	waited	5	wives	8
topic	44	undercover	55	waiter	18	wolf	8
torture	35	underground	55	waitress	23	wolves	8
total	32	underpass	55	wallet	28	woman*	8, 36
tough	47	undershirt	55	walnut	25	women	8
toward	28	unequal	48	wander	28	worker	28
tower	24	uneven	48	wanted	5	working	4
tractor	33	unfair	26, 48	warden	28	world	28
trading	3	unhappy	48	wardrobe	28	worry	28
traffic	44	unicorn	51	warmth	28	worse	28
traitor	34	unicycle	51	warning	28	worship	28
tranquil	45	uniform	51	warrior	28	worthless	54
travel	32	union	51	watch	28	worthy	28
treasure	35	unique	45, 51	watches	7	wrap	1
tremble	31	unison	51	water	28	wrapping	17
trial	16	unit	13, 37	waterfall	55	wreckage	46
triangle	51	united	51	watermelon	55	wrestle	46
tricycle	51	universe	51	waterproof	55	wrinkle	46
trilogy	51	unkind	48	watertight	55	writer	34
trio	51	unselfish	48	waving	3	writing	3
triple	51	unsteady	48	wayside	11	yearning	30
triplet	51	until*	32	weaker	53	yelling	2
tripod	51	unusual	48	weakest	53	yellow*	14
triumph	47	upon	40	weakness	54	yield	58
trophy	47	useful	21	weary	30	younger	34
trouble	24	using	3	weather	33, 56	yourself	12
trust	1	vague	43	weigh	58	zebra	23
Tuesday	21	valley	38	weird	58	zero	13
tulip	21	vary	56	when	1	zigzag	43
turkey	38	very*	38, 56	whether	56		
turtle	29	village	42	whine	1		

*A word that occurs in the top 300 high-frequency words